Golden Retrievers as Pets

The Ultimate Golden Retriever Owner's Guide

Golden Retriever Breeding, Where to Buy, Types, Care, Cost, Diet, Grooming, and Training all Included.

By: Lolly Brown

Copyrights and Trademarks

All rights reserved. No part of this book may be reproduced or transformed in any form or by any means, graphic, electronic, or mechanical, including photocopying, recording, taping, or by any information storage retrieval system, without the written permission of the author.

This publication is Copyright ©2016 NRB Publishing, an imprint. Nevada. All products, graphics, publications, software and services mentioned and recommended in this publication are protected by trademarks. In such instance, all trademarks & copyright belong to the respective owners. For information consult www.NRBpublishing.com

Disclaimer and Legal Notice

This product is not legal, medical, or accounting advice and should not be interpreted in that manner. You need to do your own due-diligence to determine if the content of this product is right for you. While every attempt has been made to verify the information shared in this publication, neither the author, neither publisher, nor the affiliates assume any responsibility for errors, omissions or contrary interpretation of the subject matter herein. Any perceived slights to any specific person(s) or organization(s) are purely unintentional.

We have no control over the nature, content and availability of the web sites listed in this book. The inclusion of any web site links does not necessarily imply a recommendation or endorse the views expressed within them. We take no responsibility for, and will not be liable for, the websites being temporarily unavailable or being removed from the internet.

The accuracy and completeness of information provided herein and opinions stated herein are not guaranteed or warranted to produce any particular results, and the advice and strategies, contained herein may not be suitable for every individual. Neither the author nor the publisher shall be liable for any loss incurred as a consequence of the use and application, directly or indirectly, of any information presented in this work. This publication is designed to provide information in regard to the subject matter covered.

Neither the author nor the publisher assume any responsibility for any errors or omissions, nor do they represent or warrant that the ideas, information, actions, plans, suggestions contained in this book is in all cases accurate. It is the reader's responsibility to find advice before putting anything written in this book into practice. The information in this book is not intended to serve as legal, medical, or accounting advice.

Foreword

The Golden Retriever is a big dog breed that has an equally big heart. It is not difficult to love one of these furry, large dogs with their smiling expressions, which is probably why they are one of the most popular pets in the United States and the entire world.

Recently, however, Goldens have been getting some bad PR for being prone to too many illnesses. But many other dog breeds are in as much danger of acquiring fatal diseases as Golden Retrievers. This certainly does not diminish their need for a loving home and family, and their capacity to live a full and productive life - however long, or short, this may be.

Whether you are still considering adding a Golden to your home, or whether you already own a Golden Retriever, it is always a good idea to know as much as you can about the breed. This book would guide you in caring for your Golden, and in creating the most ideal home life that you can for you and this furry, smiling dog.

Table of Contents

Introduction 1

   Glossary of Dog Terms 3

Chapter One: Understanding Golden Retrievers 9

   Facts About Golden Retrievers 10

      Summary of Golden Retriever Facts 12

   Golden Retriever Breed History 14

   Types of Golden Retrievers 15

      British Golden Retriever 16

      American Golden Retriever 16

      Canadian Golden Retriever 17

Chapter Two: Things to Know Before Getting a Golden Retriever 19

   Do You Need a License? 20

   How Many Golden Retrievers Should You Keep? 21

   Do Golden Retrievers Get Along with Other Pets? 22

   How Much Does it Cost to Keep a Golden Retriever? 23

   What are the Pros and Cons of Golden Retrievers? 25

      Pros for the Golden Retriever Breed 25

      Cons for the Golden Retriever Breed 26

Chapter Three: Purchasing Your Golden Retriever 29

   Where Can You Buy a Golden Retriever? 30

Adopting a Rescue Dog 31

U.K. Golden Retriever Rescues 32

How to Choose a Reputable Golden Retriever Breeder ... 33

Tips for Selecting a Healthy Golden Retriever Puppy 34

Puppy-Proofing Your Home.. 36

Chapter Four: Caring for Your New Golden Retriever 39

Ideal Habitat Requirements for Golden Retrievers 40

Supplies and Equipment to Have on Hand........................ 41

Exercise Requirements for the Golden Retriever............... 43

Chapter Five: Meeting Your Golden Retriever's Nutritional Needs... 47

The Nutritional Needs of Dogs 48

Proteins 48

Carbohydrates.. 49

Fats... 49

Vitamins and Minerals 49

Water 50

Daily Energy Requirements... 50

How to Select a Quality Dog Food Brand.......................... 53

Dangerous Foods to Avoid 55

Chapter Six: Training Your Golden Retriever........................ 57

Socializing Your New Golden Retriever Puppy 58

Housebreaking your Golden Retriever Puppy Using the Crate Training Method 59

Overview of Other Popular Training Methods 61

Chapter Seven: Grooming Your Golden Retriever 65

Recommended Tools to Have on Hand 66

Tips for Bathing Golden Retrievers 67

Tips for Grooming Your Golden 68

    Brushing a Golden Retriever's Coat 69

    Trimming a Golden Retriever's Fur 69

Other Grooming Tasks 71

    Brushing Your Golden Retriever's Teeth 72

    Trimming Your Golden Retriever's Nails 73

    Cleaning Your Golden Retriever's Ears 74

Chapter Eight: Breeding Your Golden Retriever 77

Basic Dog Breeding Information 78

Tips for Caring for the Pregnant Golden Retriever 81

Whelping Golden Retriever Puppies 83

Raising Healthy Golden Retriever Puppies 86

Chapter Nine: Showing Your Golden Retriever 89

Golden Retriever Breed Standard 90

    American Golden Retriever 91

    British Golden Retriever 93

Canadian Golden Retriever 94
Preparing Your Golden Retriever for Show 95
Chapter Ten: Keeping Your Golden Retriever Healthy 99
  Common Health Problems Affecting Golden Retrievers 100
    Cancer 101
    Joint Conditions 106
    Allergies 109
    Subvalvular Aortic Stenosis (SAS) 110
    Pigmentary Uveitis 111
    Ear Infection 112
    Obesity 113
  Preventing Illness with Vaccinations 114
Golden Retriever Care Sheet 119
  1.) Basic Golden Retriever Information 120
  2.) Habitat Requirements 122
  3.) Nutritional Needs 123
  4.) Breeding Information 124
Index 127
Photo Credits 135
References 137

Introduction

Golden Retrievers are large, golden dogs with incredibly large, golden hearts. No wonder they are considered one of the most popular pets in the world today. A Golden will stay with you through thick and thin, providing undying devotion, playful romping, and with an intelligence honed by proper training, will be a formidable companion out in the hunting field.

Introduction

And yet, a Golden Retriever is not for everyone. It can be said that Goldens are high maintenance pets - from the daily exercise and attention, frequent grooming, and the need for constant company. These are things that a Golden Retriever needs in order to thrive and live a full and satisfying life. If these kinds of daily and regular activities do not fit into your lifestyle, then a Golden is probably not the right breed for you.

But a well-cared for and happy Golden is always worth a sight - they are a beautiful breed, and you can only respect the fact that they have the intelligence, the power, and the inner fortitude to justify being called hunting or waterfowl dogs. These days, they are mostly house pets, and the working types have work that mainly centers around being sniffing or detection dogs, or aid and companion dogs to those who suffer from some disability. They are generally a calm, cool and collected breed, but they can be very persistent and stubborn when a job is set before them. Truly, the Golden Retriever is worth its weight in gold - and this large breed can weigh quite a bit!

If you are set on having a Golden Retriever for a pet, this book contains plenty of useful information to guide you - from where to purchase, how to prepare your home for the presence of a Golden, how to feed them, groom them, exercise them, and train them. You will also find lots of useful and interesting information regarding the breed's

Introduction

history and ancestry, the types of Golden Retrievers, and the different breed standards recognized by different Kennel Clubs all over the world. And finally, there are also lots of practical and pragmatic information about how to care for a Golden. Enjoy reading, and enjoy the journey of getting to know your Golden companion!

Glossary of Dog Terms

AKC – American Kennel Club, the largest purebred dog registry in the United States

Almond Eye – Referring to an elongated eye shape rather than a rounded shape

Balance – A show term referring to all of the parts of the dog, both moving and standing, which produce a harmonious image

Beard – Long, thick hair on the dog's underjaw

Best in Show – An award given to the only undefeated dog left standing at the end of judging

Bitch – A female dog

Bite – The position of the upper and lower teeth when the dog's jaws are closed; positions include level, undershot, scissors, or overshot

Introduction

Board – To house, feed, and care for a dog for a fee

Break - When the puppy's coat color changes as an adult

Breed – A domestic race of dogs having a common gene pool and characterized appearance/function

Breed Standard – A published document describing the look, movement, and behavior of the perfect specimen of a particular breed

Buff – An off-white to gold coloring

Castrate - The removal of the testicles of a male dog.

Character - The individuality, general appearance, expression and deportment considered typical of a breed.

Clip – A method of trimming the coat in some breeds

Coarse - Lacks refinement.

Coat – The hair covering of a dog; some breeds have two coats, and outer coat and undercoat; also known as a double coat. Examples of breeds with double coats include German Shepherd, Siberian Husky, Akita, etc.

Condition – The health of the dog as shown by its skin, coat, behavior, and general appearance

Conformation - Form and structure of shape and parts in conformance with breed standards

Introduction

Crate – A container used to house and transport dogs; also called a cage or kennel

Crossbreed (Hybrid) – A dog having a sire and dam of two different breeds; cannot be registered with the AKC

Dam (bitch) – The female parent of a dog;

Dominance - Displays of assertiveness of one dog over other dogs

Double Coat – Having an outer weather-resistant coat and a soft, waterproof coat for warmth; see above.

Ear set - A description of where the ears are set on the head

Even bite - Also *level bite*, meeting of upper and lower incisors without any overlapping

Ear leather - The flap of the ear

Feathering – A long fringe of hair on the ears, tail, legs, or body of a dog

Fetch - A game of retrieval

Gait - A pattern of steps with a particular rhythm and footfall

Game - Wild animals being hunted

Genealogy - Also *Pedigree*.

Gestation Period - From the time of mating until birth.

Introduction

Gun dog - Dog trained to hunt game.

Groom – To brush, trim, comb or otherwise make a dog's coat neat in appearance

Heat - Estrus, fertile period of the female.

Heel – To command a dog to stay close by its owner's side

Hip Dysplasia – A condition characterized by the abnormal formation of the hip joint

Inbreeding – The breeding of two closely related dogs of one breed

Interbreeding - The breeding of dogs of different breeds

Kennel – A building or enclosure where dogs are kept

Lead - Leash

Litter – A group of puppies born at one time

Markings – A contrasting color or pattern on a dog's coat

Mate – To breed a dog and a bitch

Milk teeth - Baby teeth

Mongrel - The result of crossbreeding

Neuter – To castrate a male dog or spay a female dog

Pads – The tough, shock-absorbent skin on the bottom of a dog's foot

Introduction

Pedigree – The written record of a dog's genealogy going back three generations or more

Point - A stylized stance of a hunting dog to indicate the location of game

Puppy – A dog under 12 months of age

Purebred – A dog whose sire and dam belong to the same breed and who are of unmixed descent

Retrieve - Bringing back game to the hunter

Retrieving Breeds - Sporting breeds that retrieve birds from water or over land

Shedding – The natural process whereby old hair falls off the dog's body as it is replaced by new hair growth.

Sire – The male parent of a dog

Smooth Coat – Short hair that is close-lying

Spay – The surgery to remove a female dog's ovaries, rendering her incapable of breeding

Stud - Male dog used for breeding

Tricolor - a coat of three distinct colors, usually black, white and tan

Trim – To groom a dog's coat by plucking or clipping

Introduction

Type - A sum of qualities distinguishing a specific breed or a specific dog

Undercoat – The soft, short coat typically concealed by a longer outer coat

Wean – The process through which puppies transition from subsisting on their mother's milk to eating solid food

Whelping – The act of birthing a litter of puppies

Whiskers - Sensory organs consisting of hairs on the sides of a dog's muzzle

Chapter One: Understanding Golden Retrievers

It is imperative that prospective owners of Golden Retrievers find out what they can about the breed's unique traits, nature and characteristics before they open up their homes to this very popular breed. It would not be mincing words to say that Goldens will be quite a demanding house pet to keep, as they will need lots of exercise, frequent grooming, space, and lots of love and attention. They will surely be worth all that investment of time and energy, but if you simply cannot devote that much of your resources or your time to keeping this new family member, then this breed is probably not for you.

Chapter One: Understanding Golden Retrievers

Below you will find a general overview of some of the interesting facts and quirks about the breed. Let me introduce you to breed with a true heart of gold: the Golden Retriever.

Facts About Golden Retrievers

The Golden Retriever is a large dog breed with a characteristic long, golden coat. They are one of the most popular family pets today, owing largely to their kind, gentle temperaments and loving natures. They are also extremely intelligent, and are naturally eager to please. This makes them highly trainable dogs, and coupled with their natural strong sense of smell and hunting instincts, are now also popularly used as working dogs, serving in many capacities such as guide dogs for people with disabilities, drug or bomb sniffing dogs, and even rescue dogs.

This breed was originally developed in Scotland - to be an effective hunting or gun dog on Scottish terrain, retrieving water fowl. Golden Retrievers are thus excellent retrievers: they will love a game of fetch, and they are also excellent swimmers. They are naturally suited to swimming, in fact, as they that beautiful long, golden coat is also pretty much waterproof, and being double-coated, also provides this breed with adequate protection against the cold. They

Chapter One: Understanding Golden Retrievers

are also very sturdy and powerful, as would be expected of a breed bred to navigate the challenging Scottish terrain. But even for all its natural skills, power and energy, the Golden Retriever is also very amiable and gentle, with a friendly and sociable temperament.

All these unique characteristics which make the Golden Retriever what it is is require a goodly investment of time, energy and money. Being large breeds, they will occupy a large space in your home - and curious creatures as they are, they will have a penchant for chewing and destruction unless they are allowed to work off their energy in regular doses of exercise. That long, golden coat also requires regular grooming and maintenance. Goldens shed, and unless their hair is brushed and combed regularly, there might be a tendency for their coats to get matted or tangled, which will be quite painful for them, and a headache to their owners.

It should also be noted that Golden Retrievers do not like to be left alone - not for long periods of time. In fact, they will want to be close to you as much as possible, and as often as possible. They are very loving, devoted and gentle dogs, which make them great family pets. As guard dogs, however, they are not very effective since they are more likely to be friends with strangers than to warn you of intruders. This means that they will need constant company, grooming and exercise - so if your lifestyle keeps you out of the house for long periods of time, with no

Chapter One: Understanding Golden Retrievers

opportunity to spend time with your dog, then the Golden Retriever is probably not the best breed for you.

One other thing that bears mentioning is the recent spate of illnesses that seem to strike at this breed. Cancer, in particular, is a very worrying concern for many owners of Golden Retrievers. But even this does not detract from the love and joy that this breed can bring into a pet owners' life. Many Goldens are in need of homes, and it is to be hoped that the current unexplained prevalence of cancer in the breed will not have prospective owners closing their homes to this beautiful breed.

Summary of Golden Retriever Facts

Pedigree: Tweed Water Spaniel, Irish Setter, Bloodhound, St. John's Water Dog,

AKC Group: Sporting Group

Types: British, American, and Canadian Golden Retrievers

Breed Size: large

Height: 20 to 24 inches (51 to 61 cm)

Weight: 55 to 75 lbs (25 to 34 kg)

Coat Length: Long

Chapter One: Understanding Golden Retrievers

Coat Texture: straight or moderately wavy; a dense inner coat that provides them with adequate warmth in the outdoors, and an outer coat that lies flat against their bodies and repels water.

Color: light to dark golden colors, of various shades

Eyes and Nose: gentle, brown eyes and a brown nose

Ears: medium-sized, pendant or hanging ears

Tail: thick and muscular at the base and follows the natural line of the croup, level or with a moderate upward curve

Temperament: friendly, gentle, trusting, naturally intelligent and biddable, active and fun-loving, patient, and eager to please

Strangers: are amiable even to strangers, do not make good guard dogs

Other Dogs: compatible with other dogs

Other Pets: compatible with other pets such as cats, and most livestock

Training: intelligent and very trainable

Exercise Needs: very active, needs daily exercise of at least one hour each day

Health Conditions: Cancer, joint conditions such as hip and elbow dysplasia, allergies, subvalvular aortic stenosis (SAS), pigmentary uveitis, ear infection, obesity

Chapter One: Understanding Golden Retrievers

Lifespan: average 10 to 12 years

Golden Retriever Breed History

One of the interesting and unique things about Golden Retrievers is their history - that is, unlike many other dog breeds whose origins and history are largely unknown, the Golden's origins and history are pretty well-documented. This is largely thanks to the efforts of the Scottish lord Dudley Marjoribanks, the First Baron Tweedmouth, who practically single-handedly developed the breed.

Sometime in the mid-19th century, wildfowl hunting was a popular sport in Scotland. And due to the peculiar Scottish terrain, there was a need for a dog breed who was adept at retrieving on both land and in the water. None of the then-existing hunting dogs were quite adept at the task, and so cross-breeding attempts ensued.

In 1952, the breeding records of Marjoribanks were published, and it contained detailed records of his breeding attempts which resulted in the modern Golden Retriever breed. The ancestors of the Golden Retriever were all sporting dogs, including a Tweed Water Spaniel, the Irish Setter, the Bloodhound, and the St. John's water dog.

Chapter One: Understanding Golden Retrievers

It can be said that Marjoribanks' vision had largely become a reality in the Golden Retriever: it was powerful and active, but gentle and trainable, with a gentle mouth for retrieving game.

The breed was officially recognized in the United States in 1925, while they were registered by The Kennel Club of England much earlier - in 1903, though they were then called Flat Coats - Golden. The official name of Retriever (Golden and Yellow) were ascribed to them only in 1911. On the other hand, the breed was first registered in Canada in 1927, based on breed imported by the Honourable Archie Marjoribanks.

It could thus be said that the three types of Golden Retrievers were based on the variations in the breed that developed among these three countries.

Types of Golden Retrievers

The three recognized types of Golden Retrievers are mostly based on regional differences as recognized by the published breed standards of the Kennel Clubs in three different countries: British, American, and Canadian. In general, however, these are mostly differences in acceptable size and weight, and certain physical characteristics. All Golden Retrievers, however, have golden coats in various

Chapter One: Understanding Golden Retrievers

shades, with the same type of temperament and personality: kind and gentle, eager to please and biddable, active and powerful, confident and amiable.

Below are some basic descriptions of what sets each type apart, but for a more detailed description of the differences in the three breed types, you can refer to the "Golden Retriever Breed Standard" in Chapter 9.

British Golden Retriever

These are the Golden Retriever breeds more commonly seen in Europe and Australia. They have broader skulls and are, in general, more muscular. The eyes are also more round than the American type.

It bears noting that outside of the USA and Canada, the British breed standard is the one used in all other countries.

American Golden Retriever

The American breed type is less muscular, with darker-colored coats, with differing physical requirements compared to the British type.

Canadian Golden Retriever

The Canadian type of Golden Retrievers generally has a thinner and darker coat compared to his overseas cousins.

Chapter One: Understanding Golden Retrievers

Chapter Two: Things to Know Before Getting a Golden Retriever

After having learned some of the more basic facts and details about the Golden Retriever breed, here follows some of the more practical information regarding what it means to own a Golden, to help you better determine whether this is indeed the right dog for you. In this chapter you will find some of the more pragmatic considerations such as the costs of keeping a Golden Retriever, the pros and cons of having one in the house, and licensing information. Later on in this book, you will find more information on things such as

Chapter Two: Things to Know Before Getting a Golden Retriever

feeding, grooming, exercise, and the possible health considerations that may afflict Golden Retrievers.

Do You Need a License?

Not all states in the United States require you to get a license in order to keep a dog. But even if you live in a region where licenses are not required, it is always advisable to do so anyway. The costs and requirements would vary per state, though generally, they cost around an average of $25, and require proof of a rabies vaccination. Dog licenses are also renewed annually, which means that rabies vaccinations must also be renewed annually.

The great benefit of keeping a license is legally-recognized proof of ownership. Should your Golden Retriever ever get lost - his identifying tags will enable others to easily trace him back to you. This increases his chance of safety and security, on top of the rabies vaccinations which are really mandatory anyway.

Chapter Two: Things to Know Before Getting a Golden Retriever

How Many Golden Retrievers Should You Keep?

The answer to this question really depends on how much time, energy, money, and attention you can spare - for having more than one Golden means more time, energy and money spent. Well, of course it does mean twice the love.

But having more than one pet is not just a matter of how many you can afford to keep. Responsible dog ownership means that you have to have the means and the opportunity to care for them in the manner they deserve. Do you have space for them to romp around and play in? Can you spare the time and energy of exercising more than one Golden an average of an hour each day? And remember these are a large breed of dogs, so they will take up a lot of space, and they will also require more energy to keep in line during their daily walks and exercises, and more time spent on training, housebreaking and grooming. It also means a lot more money to shell out in terms of dog food, dog accessories and grooming supplies, and medical bills. And these are things that are basic to caring for Golden Retrievers.

On the other hand, being such a social dog that dislikes being alone so much of the time, having at least two Golden Retrievers to keep each other company might not be

Chapter Two: Things to Know Before Getting a Golden Retriever

such a bad idea. Though when you come home to find a lot of chewed furniture sprayed over with shed hair, the backyard and the garden dug up, and perhaps even muddy pawprints having been tracked into the house, you'll probably wonder why you ever thought having more than one Golden was a good idea.

Take heart. They'll grow out of their puppyhood days soon enough, and then you'll find the golden temperament of those calm, cool and loving Golden Retrievers that has made them such popular pets the world over.

Do Golden Retrievers Get Along with Other Pets?

Assuming that socialization in his early years has gone smoothly - which shouldn't be a problem given the Golden Retriever's natural social skills - a Golden Retriever is pretty adaptable to most things - other humans and pets included. So having them coexist with another pet in the house - whether another dog breed, or even feline, should be no problem. Though given his background as a hunting retriever dog, you might want to exercise due caution if you also have smaller pets around the house, such as birds, mice, or other smaller pets.

Chapter Two: Things to Know Before Getting a Golden Retriever

How Much Does it Cost to Keep a Golden Retriever?

Being a responsible dog owner means not only being able to house them in your home, but also being able to afford their upkeep. This is one of the more pragmatic things that you can do, as the cost of dog health checkups, vaccinations, food, and various grooming supplies can really add up. You will eventually learn that having a dog in the house means factoring in their needs in your monthly and yearly budget. So how much does it cost to keep a Golden Retriever?

Expect to shell out a bit more in the first year as you will be spending for initial costs such as the purchase of vaccinations ($80-$300), spaying and/or neutering ($90-$200), dog accessories such as their beddings, water and food bowls, and leash, collar and harness ($250-$500). And of course, there is the purchase of the Golden Retriever himself. In general, adopting one from a rescue can cost you anywhere from $250-$300, while obtaining a purebred puppy from a reputable breeder can cost as much as $1,000 or more.

Aside from these initial costs, there are also the yearly costs such as food, vaccinations, and regular medical checkups. Below is a table that gives an estimate of some of

Chapter Two: Things to Know Before Getting a Golden Retriever

the yearly expenses that you might spend for keeping one Golden Retriever:

	In USD	based on conversion rate of 1GBP=1.438 USD	based on conversion rate of 1USD=1.303 AUD
License	$5-20	£3.47-13.91	AUD6.51-26.06
Estimated annual food consumption	$325-750	£226.08-521.73	AUD423.47-977.25
Grooming supplies and services	$35-250	£24.34-173.91	AUD45.60-325.75
Toys and other accessories	$100-300	£69.56-208.69	AUD130.30-390.90
Training in obedience schools	$75-300	£52.17-208.69	AUD97.72-390.90
Annual shots	$50-175	£34.78-121.73	AUD65.15-228.02
Medical care, treatment and supplements	$350-1,975	£243.47-1,373.89	AUD456.04-2573.42

Chapter Two: Things to Know Before Getting a Golden Retriever

Annual Total	$940-3,770	£653.87-2622.55	AUD1224.79-4521.4

So expect to spend around an average of $1,000 or more each year as the cost of keeping one Golden Retriever as a pet.

What are the Pros and Cons of Golden Retrievers?

So now you might be asking whether having a Golden Retriever is worth the monetary cost, as well as the energy it would take to care for them and train them. Many Golden Retriever owners will tell you it surely is, but of course this is something that each prospective pet owner has to decide on their own. Here is a brief overview of the pros and cons of the breed, which you can consider as you make your decision whether or not a Golden Retriever is the right breed for you to keep as a pet.

Pros for the Golden Retriever Breed

Chapter Two: Things to Know Before Getting a Golden Retriever

- Golden Retrievers are intelligent, very trainable, and love to please. You might surprise yourself with the sheer amount of commands they can learn, and how eager they will always be to please you. They are also very affectionate pets, and these dogs will likely be plopping themselves at your feet as you sit at your desk or sit on the couch to watch TV.
- Golden Retrievers are demanding in their exercise needs. This is a big plus for those people who like living an active lifestyle, or who are looking for a doggy partner as they strive to be more active.
- Goldens are beautiful dogs, with an equally beautiful temperament. If you come from a family with kids, and possibly other pets, this is a wonderful breed to have as they are great with kids.

Cons for the Golden Retriever Breed

- Golden Retrievers, especially the puppies will chew and swallow most things. This can mean ruined furniture, and also trips to the emergency room to remove those things he swallowed.
- Golden Retrievers shed quite a lot. Thus they will require extensive and regular grooming.

Chapter Two: Things to Know Before Getting a Golden Retriever

- Golden Retrievers are demanding in their exercise needs. For those people who are not very active themselves, or whose physical conditions cannot sustain daily exercise, this can be impossible to satisfy on a daily basis.
- Golden Retrievers do not like being left alone for very long. This can be quite uncomfortable if your lifestyle requires you to be out of the house for long periods of time.
- While it has not always been the case, in recent years, Golden Retrievers have been becoming more prone to certain diseases, the most fatal of them is cancer. There is always that chance that your dog will get sick, which means that aside from spending additional money on their medical bills, there is always the possibility of heartbreak should their lives be cut short too early. If you are getting a Golden Retriever, you might want to look into the possibility of getting pet insurance.

Chapter Two: Things to Know Before Getting a Golden Retriever

Chapter Three: Purchasing Your Golden Retriever

If you have set your heart on having a Golden Retriever for a pet, then alongside learning more about the breed comes the necessary research into where best to get one. This isn't a simple matter of just getting the nearest available puppies. Doing so might encourage breeders who give no thought to promoting the best of the breed, and who turn out litter after litter of puppies that might be suffering from certain diseases, or who give no serious thought to placing their puppies in the best possible homes. On the other hand, you might also consider adopting a Golden from a rescue, thereby giving one of these dogs a loving home.

Chapter Three: Purchasing Your Golden Retriever

This chapter contains some guides, information and resources on where you might turn in acquiring a Golden Retriever.

Where Can You Buy a Golden Retriever?

The best place to purchase a Golden Retriever puppy is undoubtedly from a reputable breeder. They will have taken the trouble to screen the parents for any congenital diseases, and would surely have taken good care of the mother and her puppies during birth and during the weaning process. This ensures a greater chance of you getting a healthy puppy with no social maladjustments.

Beware of purchasing a puppy from a pet store, even if they tell you that they only get their dogs from reputable breeders. No reputable breeder will even consider selling their puppies to a pet store, to be displayed at the window and advertised for sale.

You might want to check out your local Kennel Club - they usually provide the public a listing of registered reputable breeders in your area, and you can at least rest assured that these breeders have gone through proper selection techniques to be included in such a list.

Chapter Three: Purchasing Your Golden Retriever

On the other hand, you might consider adopting a rescue instead.

Adopting a Rescue Dog

There are far too many dogs in need of rescue nowadays - dogs with no homes to go to, and whose futures are uncertain. And you needn't always fear that you will be getting sick or traumatized dogs. Sometimes you might actually come across intelligent and loving purebred Golden Retrievers just waiting for a prospective owner to recognize their pet potential.

There are a number of rescues you might try, if you are considering this as your option for getting a Golden Retriever. There are even some rescues in the United States that are exclusively devoted to placing Golden Retrievers, exclusive from other breeds, with loving homes.

The National Rescue Committee of the Golden Retriever Club of America (GRCA) actually carries a pretty comprehensive listing of the various Golden Retriever rescues all over the United States, listed by region and state. You can check out its resources here:

Rescues listed by Region, as published by The Golden Retriever Club of America National Rescue Committee: <http://www.grca-nrc.org/localrescues.html>

Chapter Three: Purchasing Your Golden Retriever

Other Golden Retriever rescues, and listing of rescues, in the United States and the UK, are listed below:

AbsolutelyGolden.com provides a list of Golden Retriever Rescues listed by State
<http://www.absolutelygolden.com/rescue-clubs-by-state/>

Golden Retriever Rescue Resource
<http://www.gr-rescue.org/>

AdoptaPet.com
<http://www.adoptapet.com/s/adopt-a-golden-retriever>

Almost Heaven Golden Retriever Rescue
<http://www.almostheaven-golden-retriever-rescue.org/>

U.K. Golden Retriever Rescues

The Kennel Club provides a listing of various Golden Retriever Rescues in the UK>
<http://www.thekennelclub.org.uk/services/public/findarescue/Default.aspx?breed=2047>

Happy Paws Rescue
<http://www.happypawspuppyrescue.co.uk/meetteam.html>

Golden Retriever Rescue Cymru
<http://www.goldenretrieverrescuecymru.co.uk/>

Chapter Three: Purchasing Your Golden Retriever

Labrador Retriever Rescue
<http://www.labrador-rescue.org.uk/dogs.html>

How to Choose a Reputable Golden Retriever Breeder

If what you are looking for, on the other hand, is a Golden Retriever puppy, then you should be able to tell whether a breeder is reputable. As mentioned above, you should check out the AKC's listing of reputable breeders in your area. Once you have made a list of potential breeders to visit, the next thing you should do is select your preferred breeder. You can do this by contacting them and getting a better idea of what type of a breeder you are dealing with. A simple listing with the AKC is still better supplemented by your own first-hand knowledge, based on your own observations.

Here are a few tips to keep in mind as you begin contacting the breeders in your area:

- Ask questions, and be willing to answer the questions put to you. Responsible breeders are just as interested in making sure their puppies find a good home, as you are in getting a healthy puppy. On the other hand, don't hesitate to ask questions about the puppies, the parents, and their history. They will probably even enjoy discussing these things with you.

Chapter Three: Purchasing Your Golden Retriever

- Pay them a visit, and ask if you could view the puppies and the premises where they are kept. Take note of the cleanliness of the place, and even how clean and healthy-looking the puppies are, as well as their mother. Remember that Golden Retrievers are friendly by nature, and puppies will be quite lively and playful.
- Does the breeder seem to genuinely care for the puppies and their mother? One who genuinely cares for these little animals will be more likely to devote good care and attention to their needs.

Tips for Selecting a Healthy Golden Retriever Puppy

So you have selected a breeder, and have met some of the intial terms of the purchase - perhaps you have paid the required deposit to make a reservation. Remember that you cannot bring home a puppy until they are fully weaned - which is usually at 8 weeks. So all you have to do is wait until you get that call.

One of the further advantages of purchasing your puppy from a reputable breeder is that you at least have the trusted assurance that any puppy you pick will be reasonably healthy and well-adjusted. The choice of which puppy to pick then is completely up to you. You can pick

Chapter Three: Purchasing Your Golden Retriever

out the smallest one, the largest one, or even the one who seems most annoying, if you wish.

But to make sure that the puppy you are choosing is at least reasonably healthy, here are a few tips to keep in mind:

- They should be clean, active and lively as befitting the playfulness of puppies
- Watch out for signs of discharges from the eyes and nose
- You can test out the puppy's responsiveness by seeing how they react to your presence, or how they react to you as you raise a finger before them.
- Pay attention also to how they interact with their littermates, with the mother, and even with the breeder. The puppy should demonstrate a general amiability and reasonable friendliness with all.
- You can ask questions of the breeder, too, about what the puppy is like on any given day, how often he sleeps, and how eager he is to nurse and to feed. Perhaps you could gain some idea of the best ways of caring for this unique puppy.
- Spend some time making the puppy's acquaintance. See how he reacts to your touch and to playing with you. You might be surprised to find one Golden puppy actually picks you, instead of the other way around!

Chapter Three: Purchasing Your Golden Retriever

Puppy-Proofing Your Home

While you are waiting for your Golden Retriever puppy to become fully weaned, you can put your time to good use by preparing your home. Often termed "puppy proofing," this entails making sure that it is conducive to their presence and putting away or securing dangerous items or locations in your house. It is really not quite so different from child-proofing your home, except that tiny puppies will be far more mobile, and they will be able to reach places which a toddler cannot. They will also grow far more quickly.

With all this in mind, look around your home for potential dangers to your new puppy, and secure them or store them somewhere out of the way. A few things to watch out for are:

- Tiny objects or toys that your Golden puppy might be tempted to put into its mouth. Spare yourself the stress of having to bring that puppy to a vet to dislodge swallowed items: clear out the areas within his reach!
- Secure electrical cables, window cords and curtains or tablecloths that hang right to the ground. Their natural playfulness can have them pulling and tugging at these things, and sometimes they might

Chapter Three: Purchasing Your Golden Retriever

even get themselves tangled up. For electrical cables, in particular, prevent any unintended electrocution or strangling. They will probably chew on these at some point or another.

- Keep your closets closed - unless you want your puppy making itself at home in your expensive shoes.
- Secure and store away food items. Also make sure that your garbage has a secure lid and are kept out of their reach.
- In general, keep away from their reach things like medicines, household cleaners, toxic or poisonous plants, and any sharp or dangerous tools.
- Fence in your yard. Golden Retrievers are not really wanderers, but puppies will, of course, be naturally curious, and they will follow their nose. Ideally, your yard should not have a garden, either. Be warned that they will dig.

Don't stop there. Try getting down on your hands and knees and explore your home from this perspective - watch out for anyting you may have left lying around in your house, and which would naturally arouse the curiosity of a puppy. If they might pose a danger to your puppy, or if you simply don't want them messing around with it, then put it away and out of their reach.

Chapter Three: Purchasing Your Golden Retriever

Chapter Four: Caring for Your New Golden Retriever

Is your home and living arrangement conducive to keeping a Golden Retriever? These large breed dogs necessarily occupy a large space, and it would be best to know whether your lifestyle and living conditions is ideal for keeping and caring for this type of dog. In this chapter, you will find some general information regarding what it entails to keep and care for a Golden Retriever, to best enable you to determine whether this breed is right for you. It will also equip you to prepare for that glorious day when you bring your Golden puppy home.

Chapter Four: Caring for Your New Golden Retriever

Ideal Habitat Requirements for Golden Retrievers

Because of his large size and his equally large personality, Golden Retrievers need two things: lots of space, and lots of attention. They are very attached to their human masters, and they will not like to be left alone for long periods of time. If your lifestyle is one that keeps you out of the house for hours or days at a time, then you're probably going to be looking at a very unhappy Golden. If so, then this breed is probably not right for you.

They will also need lots of space. Those cute, bouncy puppies will grow large fairly fast, and soon they will be occupying a lot of floor space. A yard is a definite must - it allows your pet some space for safe romping and playing without the dangers of bumping into or destroying your furniture. Having a yard is also useful whenever it is time to groom him, or when it is time for him to shed. There will likely be a lot of shedding hair falling all over the place, but you can keep this under manageable control if you make it a practice to conduct his grooming and brushing out in the yard.

And because they certainly do not like to be left alone for long - you will have to provide them some indoor space, too. This is particularly true because Golden Retrievers are not good guard dogs. Their tendency to wander is not as

Chapter Four: Caring for Your New Golden Retriever

great as other, more independent breeds, but they are very friendly with everyone - strangers included. Unless you have a securely fenced yard, you might want to keep him inside the house during the night. He will prefer being as close to you as possible, too - or be prepared for a lot of whining and barking during the night.

This means a lot of floor space indoors. Their bed alone will need to be fairly large, and will need to be out of the way of any constant traffic of people or lights or sounds to ensure a good night's sleep for this large dog. That said, given enough regular exercise, attention, and the proper training, they are pretty well-behaved and calm dogs.

Supplies and Equipment to Have on Hand

To best be able to care properly for your Golden Retriever, there are a few basic equipment you need to have on hand, and which you need to familiarize your Golden with early on. These include:

- Crate or carrier
- Blanket or dog bed
- Food and water dishes
- Toys (assortment)
- Collar, leash and harness
- Grooming supplies

Chapter Four: Caring for Your New Golden Retriever

You will be using these tools regularly over the coures of your Golden's life, so it is best to invest in quality equipment right at the outset. The uses for each are pretty self-explanatory.

An assortment of toys, in particular, is very useful throughout the Golden's life: it gives them something to chew while they are teething, or even when they just want something to chew. It would also provide them with enough distraction when, for some reason, they need to stay indoors - for instance, unwholesome weather conditions that is not conducive for their daily walk. That is why having a yard is also important. You can play fetch with him out in your yard as an alternative to his daily walking exercise.

Make sure that his bedding is thick and firm enough so that he can comfortably rest his weight on the floor. One of the most common conditions that afflict larger dog breeds are those affecting their joints. In many instances, this can be prevented by providing him warm, thick doggy beddings with a firm support so that his bones and joints are cushioned as he lays his weight on them when he sleeps. This would also keep him from getting a chill, especially during the winter months, as when he is sleeping on a cold floor or a thin blanket, for instance.

So give him a good place to rest his weary bones, and providing he does not suffer from any genetic conditions,

Chapter Four: Caring for Your New Golden Retriever

your Golden is more likely to stay in top condition for a very long time.

Exercise Requirements for the Golden Retriever

Golden Retrievers were bred to be out in the field - going out in all kinds of weather conditions helping their human master by retrieving game such as waterfowl or ducks. They will dive right into the water to do this. Golden Retrievers nowadays are mostly family or house pets, but they still retain some of the characteristics that enabled them to do their original job: they have a thick, double coat that is also water-resistant, and they have very high energy levels.

Originally from Scotland, Golden Retrievers were bred specifically to thrive and live in the challenging terrain of the Scottish Highlands. They are sturdy creatures, with a capacity for going long distances over challenging ground in some very unfavorable weather. They were not meant to stay indoors cooped up for long periods of time, and neither were they meant to thrive on minimal physical activity. The consequences otherwise is a Golden with a lot of energy to burn that he might work off in some very destructive ways. Or else he might develop some weight problems that might seriously compromise his overall health.

Chapter Four: Caring for Your New Golden Retriever

So how much exercise does a Golden Retriever need? This will vary, of course, depending on your Golden's life stage and current state of health. But in general, for an adult Golden Retriever in relatively good health, here are a few basic guidelines to remember as you work out your pet's regular exercise schedule:

- In general, an hour's worth of exercise each day is a good average. It might be helpful if you know your dog's lineage - was he bred from a show line of dogs, or from a working field line? The latter will be the leaner types, while the former will be the fluffier, smaller Goldens of the show ring. The show dog types might be happy with less than an hour's worth of exercise each day - around 45 minutes, for instance. On the other hand, the working field dogs will be able to handle as much as two hours per day!
- Create variety in your Golden's regular exercise: some days you can just go for a simple walk, other times you can run or jog together, and sometimes you can play a game of fetch. Every so often, your Golden can even test out his swimming skills! Introducing variety into his daily schedule will stimulate his mental adaptability, as well as keep him from boredom.
- Bring him for a veterinary checkup before you embark on any kind of exercise regimen. Doing so would mean that you are fully informed about your

Chapter Four: Caring for Your New Golden Retriever

Golden's physical state, and whether or not he has a condition that too much exercise might exacerbate. You might also take the time to discuss any exercise ideas you have with your vet, and see if he approves.

- Adjust accordingly, depending on the unique needs of your Golden Retriever. If your Golden seems to tire too easily, then perhaps you are giving him too much exercise. Remember that the Golden loves a challenge, and he will love to please you - he will take on anything you dish out, regardless of his physical capacity. The best thing you can do is to pay attention - you can usually tell if it was too much exercise for him, or too little. Either he ends up with too much energy to spare, or too little.

Chapter Four: Caring for Your New Golden Retriever

Chapter Five: Meeting Your Golden Retriever's Nutritional Needs

It isn't really known to what extent the impact that dog food has on some of the Golden Retriever's propensity to contracting certain diseases, such as allergies and cancer - though needless, to say, his diet does have a direct relationship to whether or not your Golden becomes obese. It's probably safe to assume that anything he eats will have a direct bearing on his health and fitness, so it is crucial that you give your Golden the right diet, and in the right proportions.

Chapter Five Meeting Your Golden Retriever's Nutritional Needs

The Nutritional Needs of Dogs

These days, most, if not all of the food that our pets take in are the ones we choose to give them - and most often than not, these are primarily dog food. So it pays to ask ourselves "What is it, exactly, that we are feeding them?"

Many dog foods contain the following on their labels: "complete and balanced." To be able to use this statement, each package must contain a certain balance of essential proteins, fats, minerals, and vitamins, based on AAFCO-prescribed standards. Following are brief descriptions of each, and how they help to maintain your dog's health:

Proteins

Mainly obtained from meat and most meat-based products, protein is essential for growth and cell regeneration and repair, and for Goldens, are necessary in the maintenance of their beautiful coat or fur. In general, adult dogs require at least 18-25 percent of protein in their diet.

Chapter Five Meeting Your Golden Retriever's Nutritional Needs

Carbohydrates

This is usually derived from fiber-based products, and help in maintaining the intestinal health of your pet. Some carbohydrates can even be a good source of energy for your pet. Examples of these are wheat, barley, corn, and oats.

Fats

Fats provide your pet with a concentrated source of energy, and are also essential for some vitamins (A, E, D and K) to be absorbed. They help in protecting the internal organs and are vital in cellular production. Fats generally account for abou10-15 % of an adult dog's diet. Anything in excess, such as calories from table scraps and treats) may lead to weight problems and obesity.

Vitamins and Minerals

Vitamins and minerals usually cannot be synthesized by a dog's body, so the primary source of these are the synthesized versions obtainable in commercially available quality dog foods. Vitamins and minerals help in the normal

Chapter Five Meeting Your Golden Retriever's Nutritional Needs

functioning of their bodies, and also helps maintain their bones and teeth.

Water

Like humans, majority of a dog's body composition - about 70%, in fact - is composed of water. Dehydration is thus a very real danger if you do not provide him plenty of readily available drinking water on a daily basis.

Daily Energy Requirements

You might ask why it is that, if dog food is so essentially balanced and complete, that so many dogs suffer from obesity? Well, the simple answer is that the amount of dog food you give your Golden is just as important as the content of his food. It is far too easy to over-feed, and on top of the little daily treats and snacks we slip our beloved pet, those calories can really pile up!

It may sound funny, but canine obesity is actually a serious problem. Being overweight means that your dog would not be able to support his weight, thus compromising his joints and his legs and feet. Diabetes and heart conditions are also potential problems for overweight dogs.

Chapter Five Meeting Your Golden Retriever's Nutritional Needs

So how do you know just how much or how little to give your Golden on any given day? There actually isn't a simple answer to that. It varies, depending on many different factors, such as your dog's lifestyle, how active he is, whether he is sick or not, the weather, and even whether he has been neutered or not. And of course, his stage of life affects his diet, too: puppies, adults, aged, pregnant, or lactating - these things also do affect the amount of food your Golden needs on a daily basis.

The easiest thing to do is to consult your veterinarian. Together, you can plan out a recommended daily diet for your pet. After that, it would be up to you to make little adjustments - depending on your observation of your dog's daily condition. Cut back a little on the food you give him if you find him growing a bit stout around the belly, and give him a little more if he seems lethargic. Remember that you shouldn't make any major dietary changes without first consulting your veterinarian.

As a basic principle, each dog has what is called an RER, or a Resting Energy Requirement. This is the daily recommended caloric intake for your pet, calculated by his weight. For large dogs, that formula is: RER = 70 (weight in kg)$^{0.75}$

The result is the daily caloric intake your pet needs if he is resting. This base amount would change depending on

Chapter Five Meeting Your Golden Retriever's Nutritional Needs

the myriad activities he undertakes each day, or the life changes he goes through, and so giving your Golden some dog food is never quite as basic as just measuring out a standard of 2 cups or so each day. Just as you would also adjust the amount of food you take in daily based on how you feel at any given time, adjustments must also be made to your dog's daily diet. Pay attention to how he behaves, and use your best judgment. Again, remember that you should never make any major or drastic changes in your Golden's diet without first consulting a professional.

The following table shows some of the daily activities that a Golden might undertake, and the recommended adjustments to the base amount of his RER:

Neutered Adult	RER x 1
Intact Adult	RER x 1.6
Moderate Work Adult	RER x 3
Pregnant dog in the last 21 days before birth	RER x 3
Weaning Puppy	RER x 3
Adolescent Puppy	RER x 2
Obese Puppy undergoing weight loss activities	RER x 1

Chapter Five Meeting Your Golden Retriever's Nutritional Needs

How to Select a Quality Dog Food Brand

It can often be confusing - when you're out shopping for dog food, to figure out which is the best one for your pet. All the commerially-available dog food products attest to being the "best" and complete quality dog food for Golden Retrievers. But how do you really know?

Read the label. The first few ingredients on the list of are probably the most important ones - they will likely account for the greatest content inside that packaged dog food. Why? Because manufacturers are required by law to list a product's ingredients in descending order, according to their pre-cooked weights. That also means that the farther down the list you find an ingredient, the less amount of it is added into the food.

How does this help us? First of all, while dogs are essentially omnivores, they are still primarily meat-eaters, and so a meat-based diet is highly recommended. You can tell whether a certain dog food is meat-based by reading the first two or three ingredients on the label. It should contain meat rather than grain. Elsewhere on the label, you should try to choose products which do not contain any artificial preservatives or colors.

Chapter Five Meeting Your Golden Retriever's Nutritional Needs

Large dog breeds such as the Golden Retriever tends to eat a lot, so choosing dry dog food instead of canned or semi-moist would certainly be more economical. They are also easier to store. And there are also some who contend that dry food stimulates silava production which helps maintain your dog's dental health.

Ultimately, there is no one answer to all canine needs - each dog is an individual, and what works for one might not work for others. For Golden Retrievers in particular, their daily diet is of utmost importance because there is a very big chance that the recent spate of diseases and illnesses affecting the breed may be due to the commercial dog food which they are consuming. As they say, you are what you eat.

The best thing that you can do is consult with your vet, read a lot, ask other pet owners, and be observant of your Golden Retriever. Any dietary choices you make for your pet must be always be fully informed and for the best interest of your own, particular dog.

Chapter Five Meeting Your Golden Retriever's Nutritional Needs

Dangerous Foods to Avoid

Just as you should be watchful of what you feed your dog, you must also be alert as to what a dog should not ingest. Since Golden Retrievers, as a breed, do have a propensity for putting this in their mouth and chewing, you must be able to distinguish which are harmless and which are dangerous foods that your Golden should not ingest. What makes it doubly more difficult to tell is that some of these are "people foods" - or foods that we take in ourselves on a regular basis, and which we might not be aware is actually dangerous for canines.

Here is a list of some of these dangerous food items which your dog should never eat. If they do ingest them, you are advised to call emergency services immediately.

- Alcohol
- Apple seeds
- Avocado
- Cherry pits
- Chocolate
- Citrus
- Coconut
- Coffee
- Garlic
- Grapes/raisins
- Hops
- Macadamia nuts
- Milk and Dairy
- Mold
- Mushrooms
- Mustard seeds
- Onions/leeks
- Peach pits

Chapter Five Meeting Your Golden Retriever's Nutritional Needs

- Potato leaves/stems
- Raw meat and eggs
- Rhubarb leaves
- Salty snacks
- Tea
- Tomato leaves/stems
- Walnuts
- Xylitol
- Yeast dough

Chapter Six: Training Your Golden Retriever

Training your Golden Retriever might be one of the more enjoyable aspects of owning a Golden. Why? Because Goldens are eager to please animals, with the intelligence, loyalty and dedication to back it up. You will find that they excel naturally in obedience training, and have a penchant

Chapter Six: Training Your Golden Retriever

for agility and fetching games - they are hunting dogs and retrievers, after all.

This chapter contains some guidelines and recommendations for training Golden Retrievers: where to start, how to proceed, and which training methods are recommended.

Socializing Your New Golden Retriever Puppy

It's best to start them out when they're young - socialization is a way to accustom them to the presence of humans and other animals, and it keeps them calm in the face of anything new or strange. The benefits are obvious - this makes future training easier, and it allows them to live a stress-free life, without being under constant anxiety or fear should anything new or strange present itself to them or in their environment.

Socialization is really just spending time with your new puppy, and getting him accustomed to your presence. Gradually, you will introduce him to the wider world - on walks or romps in the park, where he will be introduced to new environments, new sights and smells, other humans and other animals. What he does need to learn at this point is that just because something is new or strange does not

Chapter Six: Training Your Golden Retriever

make them a threat. He can freely explore the world and satisfy his curiosity without being overly timid or shy.

Socialization should be done as soon as possible, even if it is little things like you spending time with them. Most experts agree that there is a very small window within which puppies can be socialized. Any later than 12-18 weeks, and it would be very difficult, if not impossible, to get them past the natural timidity and caution of their puppyhood days.

In addition to the socialization training, you should now begin teaching your Golden puppy a few basic things, such as their name, to come to you when you call, the use of a leash and collar, and of course, housebreaking.

Housebreaking your Golden Retriever Puppy Using the Crate Training Method

This is a popular method used for most dog breeds to teach puppies - and even adult dogs - housebreaking. They key is confining your puppy to a crate in between the times when he has to go. It assumes that first, the puppy won't want to poop or urinate in his own bed, and that you are giving him a regular schedule of feeding and drinking, and also a regular daily schedule when you take him out of the crate and bring him to the yard where he is expected to do his business.

Chapter Six: Training Your Golden Retriever

Expect this to take some time as he figures out what is expected of him. You can further support this type of training by being consistent in your responses. Remember that a puppy has no idea yet what is expected of him, and by being clear in your signals, you can clearly impart to him the rules of housebreaking: that it isn't good to poop or pee inside the crate, and that it is good to poop or pee in his designated spot in the yard.

You can use displays of affection and even treats to reinforce the good behavior, while a firm voice and withholding of affection to express your disapproval. Since one of the trademarks of a Golden Retriever is its exceptional eagerness to please, it should pick up on your signals when done consistently and regularly on a daily basis. Just be patient and consistent.

While crate training is a good foundation for training housebreaking, it is also useful in many other respects, too: it accustoms your Golden Retriever to confinement in his crate whenever you are out of the house for a period of time, for instance. And of course, it makes it easier to travel with your Golden if he has no qualms about being in a crate for long periods of time.

Allow him a roomy crate, one where he can move in freely. Provide him with a comfortable blanket and an assortment of toys to keep him happy and distracted during his period of confinement, and keep this clean and conducive to serving as his living and sleeping quarters.

And of course, don't forget to give him sufficient time outside of the crate - not just for housebreaking, but also for his regular exercise and walks. He will be more likely to stay calm and quiet inside the crate once he has had a chance to burn of his excess energy in his regular exercise.

Overview of Other Popular Training Methods

Housebreaking, learning to come when his name is called, and getting used to being on a leash and collar when you go out for your regular walks, are just the starting point for Golden Retriever training. Once you've made a success of these fundamentals, you can begin to explore the wider world of dog training.

You might want to experiment with some other basic commands such as sit, heel, lie down, sit up, play dead, roll over, and the like. You'll probably be suprised - or not - at the great number of commands and vocabulary your Golden will recognize and respond to with proper training. And you will also spend some time teaching him some negative commands - not to chew on furniture, not to jump on your bed, or not to venture where he is not expected to go - like outside of the yard or inside your bedroom, for instance. A negative response such as a firm "No," coupled with the withholding of affection for some time, might suffice.

Just don't forget to display positive reinforcement each time he does what you tell him to, and vice versa - and be clear and consistent. Remember also that your Golden

Chapter Six: Training Your Golden Retriever

wants to do what you ask him to. He just needs time to learn what you mean.

That is why it is important to be quick in your response. If too much time has elapsed, for instance, from the time when he had an accident in the crate, and the time when you display negative reinforcement, your puppy might end up becoming confused. What if all that he had been doing since then had been to play with the chew toy you gave him? He might end up thinking that your disapproval was directed towards this instead of to the little accident on the floor of his crate. After all, that had been hours ago!

Done in a positive atmosphere, each learning experience and each new trick learned will only make your puppy more willing and eager to learn more. This can be a very enjoyable experience for the both of you, and a perfect time to bond and strengthen your relationship.

A good idea, therefore, is to maximize his natural skills and abilities during his training. Golden Retrievers are natural - well, retrievers - so a good fetching game will be very enjoyable to him. Have a bag of treats handy to help in your training, though if hugs, ear scratches and belly rubs work, you might as well limit those treats. You don't want him to respond to you just for the sake of the treat, and you certainly don't want him growing obese before he has even matured!

Chapter Six: Training Your Golden Retriever

Here are a few other ideas for games that a Golden Retriever is naturally inclined to, and that you can use to support and supplement your training, and of course, to strengthen your bond:

- Being natural swimmers, fetching and retrieving via swimming is a good idea. If you have a shallow pool or lake to start out the young puppy, toss a few things like a toy out into the water and have them retrieve those items for you.
- Play find and retrieve. Try placing his favorite toy out in the yard and asking him to get it for you. Use word associations like your name for the toy (which he should be able to recognize by now), and your usual retrieval phrase like "fetch" or "get." You might even try doing this with other items like the newspaper, for instance, or other regular items around the house.
- Golden Retrievers are known for being one of the most agile dog breeds, especially during dog shows. Try it out on your pet: at first, walk him slowly through and around a course of erect sticks or low posts on your yard. You can increase the speed of this each time until he learns the course on his own. This is particularly useful if in case the weather does not permit his regular walks. In this way, he can still burn off some of his restless energy with games right in your backyard, or even inside your house!

Chapter Six: Training Your Golden Retriever

Always strive to make these training and game sessions as fun and enjoyable as possible for you and your Golden. Golden Retrievers are naturally friendly and kind, and they are quite playful, so you can also use this part of their temperament to support and bolster the success of your training methods!

Chapter Seven: Grooming Your Golden Retriever

One of the trademarks of a Golden Retriever is their long, beautiful coat. This beautiful coat, if not groomed and maintained properly, can cause all kinds of trouble - from lots of shed hair scattered all over your house and furniture - to matted hair that can serve as the breeding ground for pests and bacteria. And yet is there such a thing as too much grooming and too much bathing? Remember that even as you groom, your Golden's coat is also its protection against the elements and the weather, so you will have to know just how much or how little is too much trimming or too much bathing.

Chapter Seven: Grooming Your Golden Retriever

This chapter contains some general information regarding recommended practices for grooming Golden Retrievers, though of course your specific needs may vary regarding your dog's daily activities and the region where you live.

Recommended Tools to Have on Hand

You might want to invest in some quality grooming tools early on if you are raising and caring for Golden Retrievers. Grooming will be an integral part of the relationship you have with your dog, and it helps if the process is enjoyable for the both of you. Quality grooming tools can certainly help. Here is a list of some of the tools you will be needing to groom your Golden:

- Quality bristle brush
- Undercoat rake
- Dog nail clippers
- Grooming shears
- Round-nosed thinning shears
- Ear cleansing solution
- Dog toothbrush and toothpaste

Of course, you can always bring your pet to a professional groomer's, but it always helps to have these tools ready to hand all the same. You cannot always be

Chapter Seven: Grooming Your Golden Retriever

bringing your dog to a groomer each time he needs a good brush or a trim - which might be quite often given the nature of his coat. Professional grooming services once or twice a year is a good average, with most of the regular grooming practices done at home.

Tips for Bathing Golden Retrievers

You don't want to bathe your Golden Retriever too often. His coat is naturally waterproof - given his background as a waterfowl retriever. Too much bathing will strip his coat of the natural oils that keep in shiny and in good condition, and can even dry it out. Being waterproof, a Golden's coat is designed to repel water and dirt and debris, so too much bathing is not really necessary.

Bathing once a month is a good schedule, though if you find that his coat is getting dry, you might want to cut back a bit and increase the regularity of regular brushing. This would stimulate the production of those natural oils that help to maintain his beautiful coat. Or you can simply shift to non-soap based dog shampoo. Though don't hesitate to give him a bathe if he had been trampling in dirt or mud.

The important thing to remember regading bathing Golden Retrievers is to dry them out thoroughly afterwards. Their thick coat can actually keep in the moisture, and this is

Chapter Seven: Grooming Your Golden Retriever

not a good idea as it may cause irritation. Pay particular attention to their ears - water or moisture should not be trapped inside or it might become the breeding ground for bacteria, thus leading to ear infections. You can use towels to dry them, or a hand-held dryer set to low.

Remember also that the caution against trapped moisture or water in a Golden's coat also applies after he has gone swimming - which this breed is naturally suited for. Bathing afterwards can serve to clean his coat of any chemical residue such as salt or chlorine from his skin, and don't forget to dry him off thoroughly afterwards.

Tips for Grooming Your Golden

Grooming a Golden Retriever's coat may seem a bit overwhelming at first. You want to clean off and get rid of all that shedding hair and excessively-long feathering, but you don't want to do it too severely, either. You don't want to damage his beautiful coat, but of course you also want him looking his best. Following are a few simple grooming tips which can guide you as you groom your Golden Retriever.

Chapter Seven: Grooming Your Golden Retriever

Brushing a Golden Retriever's Coat

- Golden Retrievers will shed their undercoat with the turning of the seasons, so you will have to brush his coat regularly. This helps to get rid of the dead hair, and it also stimulates the skin to get the blood flowing and to encourage the production of those natural oils that keep his coat healthy and shiny. This will also prevent matting hair, which can eventually be quite painful for your pet.
- Goldens will shed much more after the winter season, but there will always be any amount of shed hair throughout the year. Thus it is always best to brush his coat regularly - using a quality bristle brush and an undercoat rake - as often as you can: daily, if you can manage it, though twice or thrice a week should suffice.
- Pay particular attention to some of the problem areas: behind the ears, on the tail, and the thick feathering behind their back legs and the chest area beneath the neck.

Trimming a Golden Retriever's Fur

There are some pet owners who are under the misconception that Golden Retrievers can become too hot during summer or warm weather, and so they ask groomers for a shave. But this is not advisable because their coat acts as protection from all kinds of weather. Shaving them makes them prone to all kinds of skin conditions, and even

Chapter Seven: Grooming Your Golden Retriever

those that may be brought on by temperature changes. Besides, canines do not sweat through their body - they do so through their nose and the pads of their feet, and panting can help them release heat. So shaving does not actually help them to cool down.

What you can do is regulate your Golden's activities and weather exposure so that he does not overexert himself and suffer from heat-related conditions. On the other hand, you can trim your Golden's fur to keep him spic and span and presentable, and to decrease the discomfort both of you must be feeling at all those excessively thick and lengthy hair and coat.

- Start by combing out his fur from head to tail. Remove any matted hair that you come across.
- Using the grooming shears, start by taking off a little hair at a time - it is too easy to cut off chunks of hair that would look too short in the long run. Be cautious. Think of it as trimming off the edges rather than cutting his hair.
- Conduct the procedure on a stable table that is conveniently raised so that you can have a good view of your Golden's entire body. This also helps you to achieve balance - particularly when it comes to trimming the feathering on the back legs
- Go slowly. You will probably not need to trim your Golden's fur more than once or twice a year, so take as much time as you like. He may eventually get

Chapter Seven: Grooming Your Golden Retriever

bored or restless and make it difficult for you to continue the trimming. That's okay. You can continue it on another day.

- Untrimmed, the following areas of a Golden's body is prone to excessively long or thick hair, and would be the areas you might want to focus on: the feet, hocks pasterns, neck and shoulders, his ears, and his tail.
- You can use the round-nosed shears to trim the hair around the pads of his feet, making their length even with the pads. Also trim any of the fuzzy hair that grows from the top and sides of his feet.
- Trim the hair on the outer covering of the ear to make it look neat.
- The tail should be trimmed so that it looks like a fan when it is extended.

Other Grooming Tasks

Aside from brushing and bathing your Golden Retriever, there are a few other grooming tasks that should be carried out regularly. These include dental care, trimming your Golden's nails, and cleaning his ears.

Chapter Seven: Grooming Your Golden Retriever
Brushing Your Golden Retriever's Teeth

Brushing your dog's teeth seems like one of those things that humans do just for the heck of it. But proper dog grooming also includes making sure that their teeth and gums are properly taken care of, since they are just as prone to some of the things that afflict humans: gum disease, teeth loss and teeth decay, and even bad breath. Should they somehow contract periodontal disease, it can seep into their bloodstream, making the problem worse.

You can use dog toothbrush and dog toothpaste. Since there is a great likelihood that they will ingest the toothpaste, use those that are specially formulated for canine use. As an alternative, especially if you are only starting out, you can use your finger to brush their teeth, just getting them familiar to the idea of something foreign rubbing toothpaste against their teeth. You can start with those easy to reach front teeth - simply lift the flaps of their lips to do this. Once they become more accustomed to the idea, you will eventually be able to reach their entire set of teeth. Take it a step at a time until the habit is built - just like any form of training.

That said, there are other ways you can care for your dog's teeth aside from brushing: give them chew toys that also promote dental health, for instance. Also stick with dry

Chapter Seven: Grooming Your Golden Retriever

dog food because this is better than the alternatives in terms of dental care.

Trimming Your Golden Retriever's Nails

In general, canine nails are worn down naturally by some of the activities they do regularly, such as hunting, running, digging, etc. These are not usual activities for house pets, however, so sometimes dog nails can grow too long for comfort. Long doggie nails can get caught on things, they can break, and they can even cause your Golden to walk with a limp, which can affect the rest of his body. That is why it is also essential to regularly trim your dog's nails.

Use doggie nail trimmers, and proceed carefully. The quick - or the blood vessel that supplies blood to the nails - is sometimes not so noticeable from the surface, and there is a chance that you may nick this, causing some bleeding. If this should happen, you can treat the wound with some styptic powder. Try not to let your Golden loose for some time afterwards, lest the bleeding start again.

Go slowly. Dogs usually don't like their paws being touched, much less their nails being trimmed, so you would need to accustom her first to having her toes and nails held or touched, before you actually start trimming. If you are

Chapter Seven: Grooming Your Golden Retriever

unsure or nervous, have a professional show you how it's done at first. Generally, it isn't really a very complicated process. The main challenge is in getting your pet to sit still and unmoving while her nails are being trimmed. And like in many things, it is a habit or training that is built up slowly over time.

Cleaning Your Golden Retriever's Ears

In the section on trimming your Golden's coat, you worked on trimming the excessivel long hair on top of the flaps of your Golden's ears. Now, it's time to turn our attention to the inside of his ears.

The important thing to remember is that water or moisture must not get stuck inside your Golden's ears. Because of the peculiar shape and position of the ears of a Golden Retriever, the ears are often a cause for concern. Air does not circulate correctly, and so trapped moisture doesn't dry, providing an ideal breeding ground for bacteria, and might eventually lead to ear infections.

This is one area where you can again whip out your round-nosed trimmers, to trim off the hair that is found in the ear canal. This in itself can reduce the chances of infections. Again, go slowly. Canine ears are very sensitive,

Chapter Seven: Grooming Your Golden Retriever

and it might take some time before they get used to having someone poking around inside their ears.

Always start with the outer ears before going deeper. Check if there might be odd or foul smells coming from iside the ears, in which case you shouldn't probably bring them to a veterinarian.

Use a professional prescribed ear cleaning solution. Just a few drops inside the ear, massage the outer ear so that the solution spreads, and this should loosen up any wax buildup inside the ear, which should be remove once your pet shakes his head.

Again, if you are uncertain on how to proceed, have a professional show you how it's done. It's easy enough to do once you get the hang of it.

It is recommended that the Golden's ears be checked regularly - daily, if possible, or during the regular grooming process. Doing this regularly can help to catch any difficulties early. Watch our for signs of trouble when your Golden regularly scratches at his ears, or if he keeps shaking his head or holds his head tilted towards the side.

The end result of cleaning a Golden's ears should be a dry inner ear, with any excess or long hair duly trimmed.

Chapter Seven: Grooming Your Golden Retriever

Chapter Eight: Breeding Your Golden Retriever

In this day and age, dog breeding is a huge responsibility, and it is a responsibility that covers the entire process, from the selection of the dam and stud, the mating, the care for the pregnant dam up until she gives birth, to the care and weaning of the puppies up until they are ready to be brought home by their new owners.

Even then, you have to be able to certify to the health of the new puppies, for most new owners will likely ask you for a warranty that, to the best of your knowledge, they are in complete good health. The entire process entails

Chapter Eight: Breeding Your Golden Retriever

veterinary checkups, and coupled with the time spent and the cost of feeding and care, will also cost you a pretty penny.

So if you are intending to breed Golden Labrador puppies to make some extra money, it might not be quite so simple as that. Yes, breeding Golden Labradors can be a satisfying and fulfilling experience, but you have to do it for the right reason - the improvement of the breed. And you must be confident that you can handle the financial and psychological load that breeding entails. So consider carefully before you embark on becoming a dog breeder.

Basic Dog Breeding Information

If you do not intend to breed your Golden Labrador - you might want to look into the option of spaying or neutering your Golden. This is especially useful because doing so can actually diminish the chances of their contracting certain illnesses. And it is actually recommended that you spay or neuter your pet if they have been diagnosed with a genetic illness of one kind or another. It is the responsible thing to do - to safeguard and promote the breed by eliminating as much incidence of their genetic conditions as possible. You do not want the heartbreak of

Chapter Eight: Breeding Your Golden Retriever

having a litter of puppies that may or may not be carriers of life-threatening or debilitating conditions.

But if this is a road you wish to embark on, then it is important that you learn all you can about the process to ensure that it all goes smoothly, and that all possible difficulties are kept to a minimum. Breeding dogs is really not quite such a complicated process, though of course it pays to know as much as you can before starting. And given all the challenges and potential consequences, it is highly recommended that you bring both the prospective dam and stud for pre-breeding health checks, to screen for possible health conditions.

Once that is done, the breeding process can begin in earnest. There are a few dog breeding information that runs common among all dog breeds, and these are things that you will have to know. For instance, the reproductive cycle of the female dog can be pinpointed by identifying their estrus cycle. This is when the female is said to be "in heat." Breeding during this time can maximize the chances of conception, and can happen every 6 or 7 months, or twice a year. For large dog breeds, this usually happens for the first time when the Golden is about two years old, though it can happen much earlier. It is not recommended to breed a female Golden during her time of first heat - it is better to wait until she becomes more mature to handle the stress of pregnancy and motherhood.

Chapter Eight: Breeding Your Golden Retriever

You can usually pinpoint the onset of the cycle by several signs: the first stage, otherwise called the proestrus is signaled by a swollen vulva and bloody discharge from the vagina. This usually lasts for about nine days, and it is recommended that the time be spent in socialization with the male. The female will not yet allow mating at this time, but you can keep the dam and the stud in shared quarters so that they could get to know each other. Thus, you have to have enough space and resources to house and care for the two dogs for around two to three weeks.

During the second stage, or estrus, the female will finally be ready to accept the male. This can last for about another nine days. Most consider the time of greatest fertility to be around the 11th to the 15 day after the onset of proestrus- she will be ovulating around this time. Once the female accept the male, breeding can be repeated every other day, or for two or three more matings, to increase the chances of succesful breeding. This can be repeated until the female no longer accepts the male.

During mating, the male will mount the female from behind. There will be rapid thrusts until there is penetration and ejaculation. The male and female will not separate for another ten to thirty minutes afterwards - usually they will be positioned rear to rear. This is known as a tie, and results from a lock caused by the swollen bulbus glandis of the male penis. They will separate naturally once this is over, so it is

Chapter Eight: Breeding Your Golden Retriever

not advisable to separate them during this time. Doing so might actually injure either or both of the dogs.

If successful, the female will show signs of pregnancy such as an increase in weight and appetite, and the increase in the size of her nipples. But take note that it is pretty common for some females to show signs of a false pregnancy - the only way to be certain is by confirmation with a veterinarian at around 28 days after mating - through abdominal palpitations or ultrasound.

Tips for Caring for the Pregnant Golden Retriever

Once pregnancy has been confirmed, it is time for you to settle down to taking care of your pregnant Golden Retriever. The canine gestation period will usually last for about 63 days, and during this time, special care should be taken to ensure that she stays in good health. You should bring her to a veterinarian for checkups, and discuss with the vet the proposed changes or adjustments to her diet and exercise. In general though, here are a few things you will want to do to support and accomodate your Golden's pregnancy and expected whelping:

- Increase her food intake gradually as her weight increases. By fifth week of pregnancy, she should be

Chapter Eight: Breeding Your Golden Retriever

eating about 35 to 50 percent more than her usual food intake. Do this gradually, however, in small increments at a time, of her regular dog food. Don't make any major changes or shift to other types of food without consulting your veterinarian.

- Allow for moderate exercise - less strenuous and for shorter periods of time than her regular exercise routines. Some playing or short-distance fetching before this might be appropriate, instead of long walks or runs. Don't stop all exercises altogether until about the seventh week of pregnancy, when you should probably begin isolating her. This shouldn't be too hard since she might start showing signs of increased affection and desire to stick close to you.
- Set up the whelping box and she should begin to grow familiar and comfortable with it. Ideally, it should be roomy to accommodate her and her litter, yet with low sides or rails all around so that the puppies will not roll out of the box. Keep it somewhere warm, free of drafts, and away from too much noise, lights and activity. You can line this with newspapers for bedding that can be changed easily once it becomes soiled or dirty.
- Prepare in advance the following items in expectation of the whelping: newspapers, clean towels, un-waxed dental floss, scissors, some iodine, and the phone

Chapter Eight: Breeding Your Golden Retriever

number of your veterinarian or the nearest emergency clinic.

Whelping Golden Retriever Puppies

Your Golden Retriever might begin showing signs of "nesting" when the day is nearing. She will stick close to the whelping box, and probably even to you. Labor can begin at any time, but you can recognize the signs when her temperature drops to 99 degrees or lower (the normal will be around 102.5). She will begin giving birth to the puppies any time within the next 24 hours after her temperature drops.

Each puppy's birth will be preceded by noticeable restlessness, panting and straining. If all goes well, the process should happen naturally. There will be a placenta accompanying each puppy's birth. If for some reason it does not break as the puppy is born, it needs to be opened immediately, and the newborn's nose and mouth cleaned so that it could breathe. First time mothers might not know to do this, so you should be ready to step in when necessary. The mother should also chew through the umbilical cord to free the puppy, and then begin to lick and clean the pups after they come out, to stimulate their breathing and to clean their air passages. If she doesn't do this, you should again be ready to step in by cutting the cord carefully with the

Chapter Eight: Breeding Your Golden Retriever

floss, and cleaning up the puppies using a towel. The mother will usually pick it up after she learns what is expected of her.

Be observant of the number of placentas that come out - it should equal the number of puppies. If there are less, that probably means that one or more were left inside the mother. This can cause some serious complications with the mother. Contact your veterinarian immediately if this happens.

A Golden Retriever can produce an average of about 5 to 10 puppies per litter, and the speed at which she gives birth to varies, though take note that Golden Retrievers are sometimes known for lengthy births. The entire litter can be born in a few hours, but for some, they can take as much as half a day or more, with waves of 2-4 puppies being born each time. In between births, you can assist the pups to nurse. This gives them the crucial colostrum, or the mother's first milk, which also gives them the mother's immunity. She may not want to eat during this time, but provide ready drinking water that she can drink whenever she gets thirsty.

You should have your veterinarian's number on hand in case any complications arise, in which case you should call immediately. Take note of the time when she first went into labor, and the time that has elapsed since each contraction began and the puppies arrived, since this is

Chapter Eight: Breeding Your Golden Retriever

information that you will probably be asked. Some danger signs that may warrant a call to the vet include:

- An excessively long period of time of straining where no puppy has been born. A puppy will usually be born within thirty minutes, and should not take an hour or more.
- A prolonged break in between waves of puppies, of more than 2 hours.
- Signs that the mother is in extreme pain.
- No signs of labor after the 64th day after the last mating
- When the mother passes a dark green or bloody fluid *before* the birth of the first puppy

You will sort of be acting like a midwife here, so be encouraging and supportive, and stay with her until the last puppy is born. You will not want to lose any of the puppies - especially towards the end when the mother might be too tired to lick and clean each pup.

Once finished, the mother might want to go out and pee. You might also feed her if she seems ready toystart eating - otherwise you can just give her water. Change the newspaper beddings in the crate - they will be soaked at this point, in order to keep the pups clean and warm. You might even wish to provide them with a heating pad or lamp, kept at a moderately warm temperature. Remember that the

Chapter Eight: Breeding Your Golden Retriever

puppies cannot yet regulate their body temperature at this time, and if the mother is not there, they will have no source of heat. But beware also that overheating is not good for the pups either. A good measure is to allow them a cooler place which they can crawl to if they seek relief from the heating pad.

Raising Healthy Golden Retriever Puppies

Newborn Golden Retrievers weigh about 14-16 oz. at birth (396-453 g.). They will be deaf and blind at birth, and completely dependent on the mother - and on you! Make sure that they are kept warm because they cannot regulate their body temperature as yet, and you do not want them getting chilled - which can be quite dangerous for the pups. If you are going to provide them with a heating pad, however, make sure that there is a space in the whelping box which is cooler, and where they can crawl to when it gets too hot for them.

The Golden mother can pretty much take care of the puppies at this time - nursing them, licking them to clean them, and keeping them warm. In some instances, however, the mother may have difficulty nursing all of her babies - particularly if she has a very large litter. You can then

Chapter Eight: Breeding Your Golden Retriever

supplement them with veterinarian-recommended milk, which you can administer using droppers.

Puppies grow quickly, and your new litter can easily double their weight at birth within the next two weeks. Around the third week, their eyes will begin to open, and this can be a very thrilling time. They should also be able to hear you around this time. In the next few weeks, they will be learning how to walk, bark, and play around with their litter-mates. You might have a difficult time tearing yourself away from watching all the cuteness being played out! Just remember to change the newspaper lining the box regularly to keep them and their sleeping area clean. Consult with your veterinarian about which type of food or supplements, if any, it is best to give the lactating mother to ensure proper nutrition for both her and her pups. And of course, don't forget the puppy vaccinations. They will start becoming progressively active by now, and boosting their immunity against infectious and communicable diseases is a must.

You can start weaning the puppies by six weeks, though there are some who do so earlier - at about five weeks. You can either give them puppy formula, or dry puppy food that has been soaked in water or puppy formula. There are even those who mix in some baby rice cereal. Consult with your veterinarian regarding what he recommends for weaning, and you can read up on this subject yourself - there are loads of information available

Chapter Eight: Breeding Your Golden Retriever

regarding this. The key is making the transition to solid food gradually - don't rush!

Most puppies are fully weaned by 8 weeks. Socialization should already have started by this time. If you had done your work prior to this time, there should now be ready and willing homes to take them in. If not, be ready to go out and search for good homes. Be ready to answer prospective owners' questions, just as you should also be asking questions of your own, all to ensure that the puppies are going to proper homes with owners who are willing and responsible enough to handle the puppy's care.

Chapter Nine: Showing Your Golden Retriever

The Golden Retriever is one of the most popular pets in the United States today - in fact, it is the third most registered of all dog breeds. Goldens are kind and loyal and easygoing and devoted - and they make handsome pets, especially if they are in good health and well-groomed.

Chapter Nine: Showing Your Golden Retriever

Coupled with an inbred intelligence honed by proper training, Goldens have certainly been very prominent participants in many dog shows, not just in America but around the world.

But of course, to be a show dog means adhering to the rules - and most importantly, meeting breed standards. But these breed standards are not the same in all countries. They vary according to region, one might say having developed as they regional differences between the breeds have also developed. Below you will find the general breed standards of the three subtypes of Golden Retrievers: American, British, and Canadian types.

This chapter also includes some general information on navigating a dog show, how to join, and how best to prepare your Golden - and yourself - for a show.

Golden Retriever Breed Standard

All Golden Retrievers are similar in certain aspects - their origins, their temperament, and with coat colors of yellow or golden shades. But there are breed standards according to the three different subtypes: American, British and Canadian, and each are adhered to by the dog shows and Kennel Clubs in each specific country. Below is an

Chapter Nine: Showing Your Golden Retriever

overview of these three different breed standards for each type.

American Golden Retriever

Below is an overview of the Golden Retriever Breed Standard as published by the AKC, updated as of September 1990:

General Appearance - Displays a kindly expression and an eager, alert and self-confident personality.

Size, Proportion, Substance - Males are 23-24 inches, females are 21 1/2 - 22 1/2 inches in height at the withers. Even an inch of deviation from this standard.

Head and Eyes - The head is broad in skull, slightly arched, without a prominent forehead. There is a well-defined, but not abrupt stop. the foreface is nearly as long as the skull, the muzzle is straight in profile. The eyes are friendly and intelligent, set well apart and reasonably deep in its sockets. The preferred color is dark brown, though medium brown is also acceptale.

Ears and Nose - The ears are rather short, its front edge attached well behind and just above the eye, and falling close to the cheek. The nose is either black or brownish black.

Chapter Nine: Showing Your Golden Retriever

Neck and Body - The neck is medium long and gives a sturdy, muscular appearance. The body is well-balanced and deep through the chest.

Tail and Feet - The tail is thick and muscular at the base, following the natural line of the croup, and is carried with a merry action. It should not be curled over the back or down between the legs. The feet are of medium size, round, compact and well-knuckld, wtih thick pads.

Coat and Color - The coat should be dense and water-repellent, the outer coat firm and resilient, with a good undercoat. It may be straight or wavy, and there is moderate feathering on the back of the forelegs and under the body. There is heavier feathering on the front of the neck, the back of the thighs, and the underside of the tail. The color is a rich, lustrous golden of various shades. The feathering may be lighter than the rest of the coat. Any white in the coat that is not due to age is usually penalized.

Temperament - A Golden must be friendly, reliable and trustworthy. Any signs of hostility, timidity or nervousness is usually penalized.

Chapter Nine: Showing Your Golden Retriever

British Golden Retriever

The UK Kennel Club has published its own breed standard for the Golden Retriever. Below are some of the highlights:

General Appearance and Characteristics- Symmetrical, balanced, active, powerful, and with a kindly expression. Biddable, intelligent and with a natural working ability.

Temperament - Kindly, friendly and confident.

Head, Skull and Neck - The skull is broad, set well on the neck, the muzzle is powerful. Nose is preferably black. The neck is of good length, clean and muscular.

Eyes and Ears - The eyes are dark brown with dark rims, the ears are of moderate size, set approximately level with the eyes.

Tail and Feet - The tail is carried level with the back, and without a curl at the tip. The feet are round and catlike.

Coat and Color - The coat can be either wavy or flat, with good feathering. Acceptable colors are any shade of gold or cream. A few white hairs - on the chest only - is permissible. Neither red nor mahogany colors are accepted.

Size - The males are 56-61 cms (22-24 inches), the females are 51-56 cms (20-22 inches) in height at the withers.

Chapter Nine: Showing Your Golden Retriever

Canadian Golden Retriever

The following is a general outline of the Golden Retriever Breed Standard as published by the CKC, or the Canadian Kennel Club:

General Appearance - Powerful, active, with a kindly expression and an eager, alert and self-confident personality.

Temperament - Friendly, reliable, trustworthy.

Size - Males are 23-24 inches (58-61 cm), females are 21 1/2 - 22 1/2 inches (55-57 cm) in height at the withers. Deviation from this standard of more than 1 inch is considered a disqualification.

Coat and Color - The coat lies flat against the body, and may be either straight or wavy. Moderate feathering on the back of the forelegs, with heavier feathering on the front of the neck, back of the thighs and the underside of the tail, which colour may be lighter than the rest of the coat. Excessive length, limp or soft coats are not considered desirable. Accepted colors are various shades of gold; a few white hairs on the chest is permissible though not desirable. Any white markings other than that due to age, as well as off-colour hair or black areas are considered faults.

Chapter Nine: Showing Your Golden Retriever

Head and Muzzle - The skull is broad with a good stop, the muzzle is slightly deeper at the stop than at the tip when viewed in profile.

Nose, Eyes and Ears - The nose is either black or dark brown. The eyes are friendly and intelligent. The ears are short, hanging flat against the head, with rounded tips slightly below the jaw.

Neck and Body - The neck is of medium length, giving a sturdy, muscular appearance. The body should be well-balanced.

Tail - The tail follows the natural line of the croup, and is neither too high nor too low. It is carried with merry action, with some upward curve, but never curled over the back or between the legs.

Preparing Your Golden Retriever for Show

Do you feel that your Golden is a good representative of his breed? In that case, you might seriously think of entering him in a show. These are usually hosted by Kennel Clubs nearest your area, so the first thing you should do is research - what types of shows are held, when, what are the requirements for entering, and where they are held. You might even pay a visit to one or more of these shows just to

Chapter Nine: Showing Your Golden Retriever

see what is going on and whether you think you and your beloved pet can compete. But even if you eventually decide not to enter your Golden in a show, just being around other dog lovers, specifically Golden Retriever lovers, can be an educational and enjoyable experience.

The preparations for showing your dog actually take place long before the show itself - from when your Golden is a puppy - how you have taken care of him, groomed him, raised him, and trained him. A show is not precisely a competition between dogs to show which among them is best - it is a comparison of all these different dogs, in various show types - to the official breed standard, and which one approaches nearest the ideal. But it isn't a test to see which dog is most "perfect." It is a competition, like any other competition, and Golden Retrievers are no less beautiful and wonderful dogs if they don't compete, or don't win an award.

That said, if you think that entering a show would be an enjoyable experience for you, here are a few tips to keep in mind as you prepare for the big day:

- It goes without saying that your Golden must have had some training to speak of. You will likely be giving him some orders as you put him through the paces during the show, and you will want his prompt and easy obedience to some of the most common

Chapter Nine: Showing Your Golden Retriever

commands such as Come, Heel, Stay, etc. Obviously, housetraining is also important. You don't want him going at an awkward time during the show.

- Proper socialization is important, as signs of hostility, timidity, or shyness is usually counted against Golden Retrievers. Their natural temperament is confident, kind and friendly, and this should be apparent before the judges. A good idea is to bring him to another show prior to entering him into one, just so he could acclimatize and get used to a conglomeration of people and other dogs.
- Read up on the rules and regulations of your local Kennel Club, and for each show. Are you expected to put on a performance of some sort? This would usually depend on which type of show you will be entering him into - whether conformation, obedience, or field trials. Watching another show, asking questions, and networking with other pet owners is a good way to go about this.
- Take good care of your Golden - give him his daily exercise, feed him a proper diet, groom him regularly, and of course, have him checked by a veterinarian. You want him to be in top shape for the event - and this is not something that happens overnight.

Chapter Nine: Showing Your Golden Retriever

Once the fateful day comes, here is a checklist of a few more things you should remember:

- Make sure that your Golden is well-rested and calm - neither hungry nor restless. It's a good idea to have him groomed the day before.
- Pack a supply kit that includes his food and treats, water, any medicines he needs, toys, grooming supplies, travel beddings or crate, trash bags, paper towels or rags.
- And don't forget to have your registration papers - and any formal requirements needed - with you.
- The most important thing - don't forget to have fun!

Chapter Ten: Keeping Your Golden Retriever Healthy

Part of responsible pet ownership is being ready to support your Golden Retriever - morally and financially - in case of illness or disease, and the ability to afford him the best medical treatment possible. Though most times, a proper diet, exercise, regular grooming, clean surroundings, and clean living will serve to keep your Golden healthy and active well up until he grows old. Sometimes, however, and no matter how careful you are in caring for your pet, certain diseases can just strike - particularly those whose causes are as yet unknown.

Chapter Ten: Keeping Your Golden Retriever Healthy

This chapter contains information regarding some of the more common conditions or illnesses that affect Golden Retrievers, the signs or symptoms of each, and the current state of treatments or medicines now available.

Common Health Problems Affecting Golden Retrievers

If you feed them well, give them sufficient exercise and attention, and safeguard their health with recommended vaccinations and regular veterinary health checkups, you can make sure that your Golden lives a long and healthy life. There are, however, certain health conditions to which the Golden Retriever, as a breed, is prone to. Not all Goldens would suffer from these conditions, but part of responsible pet ownership is recognizing the signs of illness when they do arise, and acting quickly by seeking professional medical help as soon as possible. Below is a list of some of the more common health problems that afflict Golden Retrievers, with a list of symptoms that would help you identify them, and the current state of medical treatments and possible cures available.

And always remember to seek professional medical advice in both diagnosis and treatment remedies. Guessing

Chapter Ten: Keeping Your Golden Retriever Healthy

can be just as harmful as not recognizing the symptoms at all.

Common Conditions Affecting Golden Retrievers:

- Cancer
- Joint Conditions such as Hip and Elbow Dysplasia
- Allergies
- Subvalvular Aortic Stenosis (SAS)
- Pigmentary Uveitis
- Ear Infections
- Obesity

Cancer

It is an unfortunate and heartbreaking reality, but the recent incidence of cancer, and death due to cancer, in Golden Retrievers is quite high - so much so that a large-scale study is already being undertaken to determine the cause - whether it is genetic, or caused by nutrition or the environment. This study, undertaken by the Morris Animal Foundation, is expected to help address the incidence of canine and even human cancer, so it is a very popular and well-supported research effort.

It will take a few more years before the study results are in, but two things seem certain: one, that more than 50 percent (61.4% according to a 1988 study conducted by the University of Pennsylvannia School of Veterinary Medicine and published by the Golden Retriever Club of America in

Chapter Ten: Keeping Your Golden Retriever Healthy

1998) of the cause of death of Golden Retrievers is caused by cancer; and two, that the Golden Retriever's previous lifespan of some 16 or 17 years has now been shortened considerably to only about 10 to 12 years - nearly half of its usual life expectancy, due to this disease.

It is interesting to note that according to the UK Kennel Club, the incidence of cancer among Golden Retrievers, based on a study conducted in the UK in 2004, is at 38.8%, which is significantly lower. This has led to the theory that the prevalence of cancer may also be affected by breed type within Goldens, and therefore genetic. But of course, this has yet to be verified by actual studies.

The cancer types can vary, though the most common types are hemangiosarcoma, lymphosarcoma, mastocytoma, and osteosarcoma. If identified and treated early, some may even be treatable. Some of the symptoms to watch out for include:

- lack of appetite
- bumps or lumps on the body
- lethargy
- odor coming from the ears
- foul breath or excessive drooling
- runny nose, especially if bloody
- vomiting and diarrhea
- increased thirst and urination
- limping or change in gait
- difficulty urinating or blood in urine
- straining to defecate or ribbon-like stools

Chapter Ten: Keeping Your Golden Retriever Healthy

Not all manifestations of the above symptoms automatically means cancer, and not all cancer can manifest in the symptoms listed above. There are also different types of canine cancer which can afflict Golden Retrievers, and they can differ in their manifestations, severity and prescribed treatments.

Below is a brief description of most of the common types of cancer afflicting Golden Retrievers:

Hemangiosarcoma

This is a rapidly developing and highly invasive type of sarcoma affecting the lining of the blood vessels, and most casualties are caused by the rupturing of the tumor, thus causing bleeding that may result in death.

Symptoms may include loss of appetite, lethargy or collapse, weakness and weight loss, or irregular heartbeats. Affecting mostly internal organs such as the heart, the spleen or the liver, it is usually not detected until after the tumor has grown quite large or has spread. If it affects non-visceral organs, however, such as the skin, it can still be treated with surgery. If removal of the affected organ is not feasible, chemotherapy may be a possible treatment option, though it is not a cure. At most, it can possibly prolong life by about 5-7 months. This disease, unfortunately, is almost always fatal.

Chapter Ten: Keeping Your Golden Retriever Healthy

Lymphosarcoma

Lymphosarcoma is cancer affecting the lymphocites and lymphoid tissues, which are present in various types of the body such as the spleen, liver, lymph nodes, the bone marrow, and the gastrointestinal tract.

There are several ways to verify a diagnosis of Lymphosarcoma, which includes biopsy, blood count, urinalysis, and an abdominal ultrasound. These tests will also help determine which treatment is best for your Golden Retriever.

Generally, however, chemotherapy is the more common treatment, and up to 80% of those treated will go into remission. This does not mean that the cancer will be cured, but detectable cancer will at least disappear. Chemo treatments are expected to continue even beyond this stage to keep the cancer under control, but at least it means the possibility of a better quality of life for your Golden Retriever. Be aware that this treatment may also cause some serious side effects to the dog, such as loss of appetite, diarrhea, vomiting, and hair loss, though it seems that this only affects 5-10% of dogs who undergo chemotherapy.

Mastocytoma

Mastocytoma is a type of cancer that affects the mast cells, which are found in the connective tissues, mainly in the vessels and nerves closest to the external surfaces like the skin, nose and mouth. Symptoms may include tumors on or under the skin, the appearance of which can vary considerably. Some may look like a large mass, but some

Chapter Ten: Keeping Your Golden Retriever Healthy

may look only like an insect bite. Other possible signs are redness of the skin, itchy or inflamed patches, or enlarged lymph nodes. This may or may not be accompanied by vomiting, diarrhea, or loss of appetite.

Given the variations in the symptoms, the only real way to be certain whether or not your Golden has mastocytoma is a biopsy. Surgery is a possible treatment, and when performed early, may even catch the disease before it spreads. Most times, complete surgical removal of the tumor is possible, though if not feasible, then chemotherapy is usually recommended.

Osteosarcoma

Osteosarcoma is a bone tumor, and can be a painful disease for dogs since this disease basically destroys the bone. The precise cause is still unknown, though genetics and sometimes external factors like radiation, carcinogens or foreign bodies are sometimes influential.

Golden Retrievers with osteosarcoma might display symptoms like lameness, frequent susceptibility to fractures, and a swelling in the affected area, and the pain felt will be visible. This might lead to other difficulties likeaggression, whimpering, loss of appetite, sleeplessness and a refusal to exercise.

Diagnosis of this condition is done through a biopsy and other examinations. Some of the recommended treatments are amputation of the affected limb, or sometimes limb-sparing surgery where the diseased bone is replaced by a metal implant or bone grafts. This is followed by

Chapter Ten: Keeping Your Golden Retriever Healthy

chemotherapy a few weeks later to address any of the cancer cells that may still have been left behind.

Needless to say, both before and after surgery, the dog will have a limited range of motion. It is also necessary to have periodic checkups to monitor the dog's condition.

On the average, prognosis after treatment is approximately one year, sometimes less if surgery is not followed by chemotherapy.

Joint Conditions

Many large breeds of dogs are prone to some form of joint disease, likely because of their weight and the heavy daily activities they undertake, though some are more susceptible or predisposed due to genetics. But even if your Golden Retriever has no genetic joint condition, his lifestyle - including daily activities and diet - can also impact the chances of his getting some form of joint disease during his lifetime.

Examples of non-genetic joint conditions can include fractures caused by injuries or trauma, athritis, or joint conditions caused by obesity. Some of the more common manifestations include limping, stiffness, the favoring of one limb over another, a reluctance to move or exercise, and in some instances, noticeable pain.

Chapter Ten: Keeping Your Golden Retriever Healthy

On the other hand, some of the genetic or congenital conditions, which some Golden Retrievers have been found to be prone to, include the following:

Hip Dysplasia

This is characterized by a poor development of the ball and socket joint in the hips, whether in the form and structure of the femur or the socket in the pelvis, or in strength of the connective tissue and ligaments. As a result, the two bones cannot move as smoothly together as they should.

This can affect one or both of the hips, and can manifest in an altered gait or a refusal to move their rear legs. With early and proper treatment, some dogs with milder conditions may still be able to recover movement in their limbs.

Elbow Dysplasia

Elbow Dysplasia consists of abnormal development in the elbow joints, and is more common among fast-growing puppies of large breeds. It can consist of any of the following conditions:

- Osteochondrosis - abnormal development in the bone and cartilage in the elbow joints
- Fragmentation of the medial coronoid process (FMCP) - a breaking up or degeneration of the bone in the ulna

- Ununited anconeal process (UAP) - joint instability resulting from the looseness of the anconeal process, by which the humerus and the ulna cannot interact correctly
- Elbow incongruity - caused by differing rates of growth between the two bones, the radius and the ulna, causing wear and tear on the cartilage, or overloading and thus fragmentation, or other abnormalities

It is best to bring your Golden puppy for a professional medical examination for appropriate diagnosis, since the symptoms - such as a limp in the forelegs, favoring one leg over the other, or putting no weight on the leg at all - may only mimic the signs of elbow dysplasia. Radiographs taken during x-rays can confirm the presence of the condition, and help you identify the specific condition and its severity. Treatment will vary depending on what type of abnormality is present, and can range from therapeutic exercise to surgery.

Generally, once the puppy reaches 12 to 18 months, the condition will become less severe, though caution should still be taken regarding the Golden's diet, exercise, and lifestyle for the rest of his life in order not to exacerbate the condition. There is also a greater chance that he might suffer from athritis as he grows older.

Chapter Ten: Keeping Your Golden Retriever Healthy

Allergies

Allergies are usually inherited conditions, though the type of allergy and the cause (or allergen) can vary. The symptoms can range from itching, redness and hairlessness to vomiting, sneezing, and diarrhea. The only way to be certain is to get a professional diagnosis from your veterinarian, and being genetic, the only effective cure is the elimination of contact with the identified allergen. Many times, however, there are topical treatments and medicine available to relieve the symptoms.

Some allergies can manifest early in Golden puppies, though sometimes it can just happen, without any warning, later in life.

Golden Retrievers are prone to about 4 types of allergies:

1. Flea allergies- when you find your Golden scratching and itching excessively, it could be due to a flea allergy. This is quite common, and there are a number of products available to help you treat your pet and also control the flea population in the external environment. As with most allergies, eliminating contact with the allergen is the most feasible solution - which you can do by using many of the modern products available to combat fleas.
2. Food allergies - if your Golden Retriever is suffering from a food allergy, then changing the diet patterns is the solution. With the help of your vet, you should be able to identify which ingredient your Golden is

Chapter Ten: Keeping Your Golden Retriever Healthy

allergic to - many times, it could be soy beef, wheat, dairy, or poultry products. One good way you can help to identify and combat this condition is by taking careful note - sometimes even making detailed records - of the diet content of your pet, particularly during those instances before he suffers from an allergic reaction. This would help your veterinarian narrow down the cause of the allergies.

3. Atopy - this type of allergy affects the skin of the Golden Retriever, after he comes into contact with a particular substance such as spores, weeds or pollen, which he either inhales or soaks up through his skin. There might be itching on different parts of his body, and if left untreated, could suffer from redness, thickening, or even infection. Be watchful of your Golden's ears, face, feet, underarms and groin, which are the areas mmost affected. Treatment consists of specialized shampoos or sprays, and antibiotics.

4. Contact allergies - most often caused by chemicals found in household cleaners and solutions, also pollen, this can cause hairlessness in the Golden Retriever's paws, belly and underarms. This might also lead to some other types of allergies such as flea allergies or atopy.

Subvalvular Aortic Stenosis (SAS)

This is a congenital heart condition, which consists of a narrowing in the aorta that carries blood away from the heart, thus creating a turbulent blood flow. This is a tricky

Chapter Ten: Keeping Your Golden Retriever Healthy

disease to catch, and usually only after a heart murmur begins to manifest, and it is not always easy to distinguish it from heart murmurs caused by natural exercise activities. It is typically accompanied by weakness, heat intolerance, fainting or collapsing. In some cases, there are no other signs.

Screening for SAS can take place at around 16 weeks, though it is advisable to screen after your Golden is at least a year old because the development of this condition cannot really be ruled out prior to that time.

This is because the stenosis, a tissue that forms a ring below the aorta can still grow as the puppy grows older. It is this ridge that blocks or obstructs the blood flow through the aorta, which is what causes the condition. The heart works harder to push the blood through the narrow opening, and over time may have a deleterious effect on the heart and the blood and oxyen supply in the body. This can lead to irregular heart beats, fainting spells, and in some cases, even sudden death.

Treatment can consist of lessened exercise combined with beta blockers to slow the heart rate, though now there are surgical operations available to treat this condition, and has had good and promising results.

Pigmentary Uveitis

Also called Golden Retriever Uveitis (GRU), this is a breed-specific condition which afflicts Golden Retrievers.

Chapter Ten: Keeping Your Golden Retriever Healthy

The cause of this disease is presently unknown. It affects the uveal tract of the eye, which includes the iris, the ciliary body, and the choroid.

Only one eye is initially affected, and the signs are not easy to detect. Symptoms include squinting, tearing, redness, sensitivity to light, and a cloudiness in the eye. One distinctive sign of the disease is pigmentation in a "spoke-wheel" pattern of the lens, or a darkening of the iris caused by small substances filled with fluid.

This condition can eventually lead to other complication such as cataracts, glaucoma, and even blindness. Vision loss is usually a result of one or both of these complications. But take note that Golden Retrievers can also be prone to developing either cataract or glaucoma independently of pigmentary uveitis.

Possible treatment consists of anti-inflammatories that would prevent or delay glaucoma. If caught early enough, regular medical treatment can even help in maintaining the Golden's vision for a number of years. In some instances, surgery might also be available.

Ear Infection

If your Golden Retriever is exhibiting any of the following symptoms: scratching at his ear, shaking his head, or holding his head tilted to one side, it is possible that he might have an ear infection. Try to check inside his ears: if they look swollen or feel painful to the dog to have his ears

Chapter Ten: Keeping Your Golden Retriever Healthy

held, or if they are warm to the touch and show dark buildup inside the ears, then he probably does have an ear infection.

Golden Retrievers are susceptible to contracting this condition because the unique shape and placement of their ears - dangling ears that have profuse hair. As a result, air cannot circulate properly, and any moistness inside is kept from drying out, making it an ideal environment for bacterial growth.

Regular grooming should therefore include a careful cleaning of the ears. This regular examination and checking of your Golden's ears will usually solve most problems since any infection will be caught early enough to be treated. Otherwise, infections that are left undetected and untreated for some time can become chronic and might even lead to swelling and other, more severe conditions.

Consult with your veterinarian if your Golden develops any of the symptoms listed above. Depending on the kind and cause of the infection, various medical treatments and antibiotics are usually prescribed.

Obesity

Obesity has been a growing concern among dogs in recent years, not just for Golden Retrievers. And it is a serious concern because it can lead to many other debilitating conditions, such as diabetes, arthritis, damage to joints, soft tissues and bones, digestive conditions, a lowered

Chapter Ten: Keeping Your Golden Retriever Healthy

immune system, heart diseases, high blood pressure, and even cancer.

And yet, more often than not, this condition is preventable - if the Golden Retriever has been on a proper diet and regular exercise.

Golden Retrievers, in particular, were meant to be active dogs hunting out in the field, retrieving fowl or game by swimming or running. Their peculiar physique needs exercise and the opportunity to work off his great supply of excess energy. Needless to say, overeating, and the habit of eating lots of treats on top of a full day's worth of meals - and a lack of exercise, would lead your Golden to steadily put on those pounds.

Make small changes as necessary in your pet's diet and exercise regime in case you find him growing a bit heavier. Take him for his regular veterinary checkup and monitor his weight statistics. And always remember that you should never make any major changes in either his diet or exercise without first consulting with a professional.

Preventing Illness with Vaccinations

If the possibilities of the diseases above seem disheartening, take heart that the veterinary medical field is constantly seeking to combat canine illness. Many life-threatening diseases, in fact, have ceased to become so with

Chapter Ten: Keeping Your Golden Retriever Healthy

the development of vaccinations that are now routinely available to all. Some of the diseases or conditions for which vaccinations now exist include:

- Rabies
- Canine Hepatitis/Adenovirus
- Parvovirus
- Canine distemper
- Lyme Disease
- Kennel Cough
- Coronavirus
- Giardiasis
- Measles
- Leptospirosis

That is why it is so important to bring your puppy to the veterinarian as soon as possible, before being exposed to other dogs and other environmental stimuli. Aside from the natural immunity that the puppy gets from his mother through the milk, the little Golden Retriever puppy's immune system is not yet fully developed.

Below is a table listing the vaccines for specific conditions and the recommended age at which the shot is to be administered. There is also a current debate on the necessity of annual booster shots. It is always best to consult with your veterinarian so you can make an informed decision regarding this.

Chapter Ten: Keeping Your Golden Retriever Healthy

Age	Vaccination
5 weeks	Parvovirus
6 and 9 weeks	Combination vaccine (for adenovirus, hepatitis, distemper, parainfluenza, and parvovirus); also coronavirus and leptospirosis when necessary in the region
12 weeks	Rabies
12-16 weeks	Combination vaccine (for adenovirus, hepatitis, distemper, parainfluenza, and parvovirus); also coronavirus, leptospirosis, and lyme disease
Boosters	Combination vaccine (for adenovirus, hepatitis, distemper, parainfluenza, and parvovirus); also coronavirus, lyme disease, and rabies

Chapter Ten: Keeping Your Golden Retriever Healthy

Take note that of the booster shots, the only one really required is vaccination against rabies, unless the regional conditions in your area require otherwise.

Also remember that the above schedule is only a recommendation - the precise shots for your puppy, the doses and at which age it is best to be administed - will be recommended by your veterinarian based on your specific conditions.

Chapter Ten: Keeping Your Golden Retriever Healthy

Golden Retriever Care Sheet

This final section summarizes many of the important points contained in this book, giving you a brief but succinct overview of many of the essential details you will want to know as you're deciding whether or not the Golden Retriever is the right dog for you. It also provides you a handy reference guide to the essentials of taking care of a

Golden Retriever Care Sheet

Golden Retriever, such as pointers for diet and nutrition, grooming, habitat, and exercise requirements. While these points have been discussed in detail throughout the book, this Golden Retriever Care Sheet allows you to skim through the main facts and find the information you are looking for more quickly and easily.

1.) Basic Golden Retriever Information

Pedigree: Tweed Water Spaniel, Irish Setter, Bloodhound, St. John's Water Dog,

AKC Group: Sporting Group

Types: British, American, and Canadian Golden Retrievers

Breed Size: large

Height: 20 to 24 inches (51 to 61 cm)

Weight: 55 to 75 lbs (25 to 34 kg)

Coat Length: Long

Coat Texture: straight or moderately wavy; a dense inner coat that provides them with adequate warmth in the outdoors, and an outer coat that lies flat against their bodies and repels water.

Color: light to dark golden colors, of various shades

Golden Retriever Care Sheet

Eyes and Nose: gentle, brown eyes and a brown nose

Ears: medium-sized, pendant or hanging ears

Tail: thick and muscular at the base and follows the natural line of the croup, level or with a moderate upward curve

Temperament: friendly, gentle, trusting, naturally intelligent and biddable, active and fun-loving, patient, and eager to please

Strangers: are amiable even to strangers, do not make good guard dogs

Other Dogs: compatible with other dogs

Other Pets: compatible with other pets such as cats, and most livestock

Training: intelligent and very trainable

Exercise Needs: very active, needs daily exercise of at least one hour each day

Health Conditions: Cancer, joint conditions such as hip and elbow dysplasia, allergies, subvalvular aortic stenosis (SAS), pigmentary uveitis, ear infection, obesity

Lifespan: average 10 to 12 years

2.) Habitat Requirements

Recommended Accessories: crate, dog bed, food/water dishes, treats, toys, collar, leash, identification tag, harness, grooming supplies

Collar and Harness: sized by weight

Grooming Supplies: brush, shampo, toenail clippers

Grooming Frequency: groom at least once a week, and every day during heavy shedding which happens at least twice a year

Energy Level: very high, originally bred as a hunting retriever dog

Exercise Requirements: at least an hour or more of exercise per day

Crate: highly recommended

Crate Size: just large enough for dog to lie down and turn around comfortably

Crate Extras: lined with blanket or plush pet bed

Food/Water: stainless steel or ceramic bowls, clean daily

Toys: start with an assortment, see what the dog likes; include some mentally stimulating toys

Golden Retriever Care Sheet

Exercise Ideas: retrieval games such as fetching, agility exercises such as flyball or swimming

3.) Nutritional Needs

Nutritional Needs: water, protein, carbohydrate, fats, vitamins, minerals

RER: 70 (weight in kg)$^{0.75}$

Calorie Needs: varies by age, weight, and activity level; RER modified with activity level

Amount to Feed (puppy): 4 meals a day, reducing to 3 meals a day after 3 months, and 3 meals after six months, at regular intervals

Amount to Feed (adult): consult recommendations on the package; calculated by weight

Important Ingredients: fresh animal protein (chicken, beef, lamb, turkey, eggs), digestible carbohydrates (rice, oats, barley), animal fats

Important Minerals: calcium, phosphorus, potassium, magnesium, iron, copper and manganese

Important Vitamins: Vitamin A, Vitamin A, Vitamin B-12, Vitamin D, Vitamin C

Golden Retriever Care Sheet

Look For: AAFCO statement of nutritional adequacy; protein at top of ingredients list; no artificial flavors, dyes, preservatives

4.) Breeding Information

Age of First Heat: around two years old, sometimes earlier

Heat (Estrus) Cycle: 14 to 21 days

Frequency: twice a year, every 6 to 7 months

Greatest Fertility: 11 to 15 days into the cycle

Gestation Period: 59 to 63 days

Pregnancy Detection: possible after 21 days, best to wait 28-30 days before exam

Feeding Pregnant Dogs: maintain normal diet until week 5 or 6 then slightly increase rations by 20 to 50 percent for the last five weeks

Signs of Labor: body temperature drops below normal 100° to 102°F (37.7° to 38.8°C), may be as low as 98°F (36.6°C); dog begins nesting in a dark, quiet place

Contractions: ten to thirty minutes, in waves of an hour or so each time

Golden Retriever Care Sheet

Whelping: may last anywhere from a few hours to half a day or more

Puppies: born with eyes and ears closed; eyes open at 3 weeks, teeth develop at 10 weeks

Litter Size: average 5 to 10 puppies

Size at Birth: 14-16 oz.

Weaning: supplement with controlled portions of moistened puppy food at 3-5 weeks, with water freely available, fully weaned at 5-6 weeks

Socialization: start as early as possible to prevent puppies from being nervous as an adult, preferably before 14-16 weeks of age

Golden Retriever Care Sheet

Index

A

AAFCO	124
Age of First Heat	124
AKC Breed Standard	91
AKC Group	12, 120
Alcohol	55
Allergies	101, 109, 155, 157
American Golden Retriever	5, 7, 16, 91
Amount to Feed	123
annual costs	24, 25
Apple seeds	55
Avocado	55

B

Basic Dog Breeding Information	78
Basic Golden Retriever Information	8, 120
bathing	67
bed	41, 122
Blanket or dog bed	41
bowls	122
Breed Size	12, 120
Breed Standard	4
breeders	33, 34
breeding	77, 124
British Breed Standard	16
British Golden Retriever	16, 93
Brushing a Golden Retriever's Coat	69
Brushing a Golden Retriever's Teeth	72
bumps or lumps on the body	102

C

Calorie Needs	123

Canadian Breed Standard	94
Canadian Golden Retriever	8, 12, 17, 94, 120
Cancer	8, 12, 13, 101, 102, 103,, 104, 121, 158
Canine distemper	115
Canine Hepatitis/Adenovirus	115
carbohydrates	49, 123
carrier	41
Cherry pits	55
chewing	26
Chocolate	55
Citrus	55
Cleaning Your Golden Retriever's Ears	74, 75, 102
Coat and Color	12, 13, 93, 120
Coconut	55
Coffee	55
Collar and Harness	41, 122
combination vaccine	116
Common Health Conditions	100, 101
congenital conditions	107
Cons for the Golden Retriever Breed	26
Contractions	85, 124
Coronavirus	115
costs	24, 25, 33
crate	41, 122

D

Daily Energy Requirements	50
Dangerous Foods	55
dental care	73
diagnosis and treatment	101
diet	124
difficulty urinating or blood in urine	102
dog food	53

E

Ear cleansing solution	66
Ear Infection	101, 112

ears	121, 125
Ears and Nose	91
Elbow Dysplasia	101, 107, 154
Energy Level	122
Exercise	13, 26, 27, 43, 121, 122, 123
Eyes and Ears	93
Eyes and Nose	121

F

Facts About Golden Retrievers	5, 10
fats	49, 123
Feathering	5
Feeding Pregnant Dogs	124
female	3, 5, 6, 7
food	41, 122
Food/Water bowls	122
foul breath or excessive drooling	102
Fragmentation of the medial coronoid process (FMCP)	107

G

games	63
Garlic	55
General Appearance	91, 93, 94
Gestation Period	124
Golden Retriever Breed Standard	90, 91, 94
Golden Retriever Care Sheet	119, 120
Grapes/raisins	55
Greatest Fertility	124
grooming	65, 66, 68, 70, 71, 122
Grooming shears	66
Grooming supplies	24, 41, 42, 66, 122

H

habitat	40, 43, 122
harness	122

Head and Muzzle	95
Head, Skull and Neck	93
health	99, 114
Health Conditions	13, 121
Heat	6, 124
Height	12, 120
Hemangiosarcoma	103, 157
Hip Dysplasia	6, 107, 157
history	14, 15
housebreaking	59

I

increased thirst and urination	102
ingredients	124

J

Joint Conditions	8, 101, 106

L

lack of appetite	102
Leash	6, 41, 122
Leptospirosis	115
lethargy	102, 103
license	20
Lifespan	14, 121
limping or change in gait	102
Litter Size	125
Lyme Disease	115
Lymphosarcoma	104, 158

M

Macadamia nuts	55

Mastocytoma	104
Measles	115
Milk and Dairy	55
minerals	123
Mushrooms	55
Mustard seeds	55

N

Neck and Body	92, 95
Nose, Eyes and Ears	95
Nutritional Needs	47, 48, 123

O

Obesity	101, 113, 156, 158
Onions/leeks	55
Osteochondrosis	107
Osteosarcoma	105, 158
Other Dogs	13, 121
other pets	22

P

Parvovirus	115, 116, 125
Peach pits	55
Pedigree	7, 12, 120
Pigmentary Uveitis	8, 101, 111, 158
Point	7
Bite	3
Potato leaves/stems	56
pregnancy	81
Pregnancy Detection	124
Preparing for Show	8, 95, 97, 98
Pros for the Golden Retriever Breed	25
protein	48, 123, 124
Puppies	34, 35, 37, 123, 125

Puppy-Proofing	36
puppy responsiveness	35
purchasing a golden retriever	29, 30

Q

Quality bristle brush	66

R

Rabies	115, 116
Raw meat and eggs	56
RER	51, 52, 123
Rescues	31, 32, 33
Rhubarb leaves	56
Round-nosed thinning shears	66

S

Salty snacks	56
Screening for SAS	111
Double Coat	5
Shedding	7, 26
show	89, 90, 96
Signs of Labor	124
Size	91, 93, 94
Size at Birth	125
Socialization	35, 36, 58, 125
spay	6, 7
Strangers	13, 121
Subvalvular Aortic Stenosis (SAS)	8, 101, 110
Summary of Golden Retriever Facts	5, 12
supplies	41, 122
swimming	63

T

Tail	13, 71, 93, 95, 121
Tea	56
teeth	3, 125
Temperament	13, 22, 26, 92, 93, 94, 121
temperature	124
Tomato leaves/stems	56
tools	41, 66
toys	36, 41, 122
Training	13, 57, 58, 59, 61, 121
trimming hair	69, 70, 71
Trimming Nails	73
Types	12, 15, 16, 120

U

UK Breed Standard	93
U.K. Golden Retriever Rescues	32
undercoat	4, 8
undercoat rake	66, 122
Ununited anconeal process (UAP)	108

V

Vaccination	114, 116, 117, 124
vitamins and minerals	49, 123
vomiting and diarrhea	102

W

Walnuts	56
Water	12, 14, 41, 50, 120, 122, 123
Weaning	125
weight	12, 51, 120, 122, 123
Whelping	8, 83, 125

X

Xylitol   56

Y

Yeast dough   56

Photo Credits

Cover Page Photo By Звезда Севера via Wikimedia Commons.
<https://commons.wikimedia.org/wiki/File:Golden_Retriever_Yardie.jpg>

Page 1 Photo by Mauser via Wikimedia Commons.
<https://commons.wikimedia.org/wiki/File:Golden_retriever_lenndog.jpg>

Page 9 Photo by Charles-Axel Dein via Wikimedia Commons.
<https://commons.wikimedia.org/wiki/File:Golden_retriever-026.JPG>

Page 19 Photo By Barras via Wikimedia Commons.
<https://commons.wikimedia.org/wiki/File:A_Golden_Retriever-3_%28Barras%29.JPG>

Page 29 Photo by Stefan Bauer via Wikimedia Commons.
<https://commons.wikimedia.org/wiki/File:Golden_Retriever_10weeks.jpg>

Page 39 Photo by Alann via Wikimedia Commons.
<https://commons.wikimedia.org/wiki/File:Mi_Golden_Retriever.jpg>

Page 47 Photo by Catherin 888 via Wikimedia Commons. <https://commons.wikimedia.org/wiki/File:Odie-the-Golden-Retriever.JPG>

Page 57 Photo by Luizmo via Wikimedia Commons. <https://commons.wikimedia.org/wiki/File:Shara.golden.retriever.jpg>

Page 65 Photo by Akaporn Bhothisuwan from Los Angeles, USA. <https://www.flickr.com/photos/akaporn/402220960/>, as uploaded to Wikimedia Commons. <https://commons.wikimedia.org/wiki/File:Golden_Retrievers_dark_and_light.jpg>

Page 77 Photo by Gslyon via Wikimedia Commons. <https://commons.wikimedia.org/wiki/File:Golden_Retrievers_Cali_and_Katie.jpg>

Page 89 Photo by Dirk Vorderstraße via Wikimedia Commons. <https://commons.wikimedia.org/wiki/File:Golden_retriever_ruede.jpg>

Page 99 Photo by Newyorker10021 via Wikimedia Commons. <https://commons.wikimedia.org/wiki/File:GoldenRetriever Snow.jpg>

Page 119 Photo by Hooliganath via Wikimedia Commons. <https://commons.wikimedia.org/wiki/File:Golden_Retriever_Bud.JPG>

References

"13 Things to Consider Before Buying a Golden Retriever." Marley. <http://hubpages.com/animals/13-Things-To-Consider-Before-Buying-A-Golden-Retriever>

"AKC Breed Standard: Official Standard of the Golden Retriever." GRCA <AKC. https://www.grca.org/about-the-breed/akc-breed-standard/>

"Breed Standard." The (UK) Kennel Club. <http://www.thekennelclub.org.uk/services/public/breed/standard.aspx?id=2047>

"Breeding Your Dog." Cindy Moore. <http://www.k9web.com/dog-faqs/breeding.html>

"Canine Nutrition Basics." Claudia Kawczynska. <http://thebark.com/content/canine-nutrition-basics>

"Canine Pregnancy Care." all about goldens. <http://www.all-about-goldens.com/canine-pregnancy.html>

"Causes and Management of Arthritis & Other Joint Diseases in Dogs." Drs. Foster & Smith. <http://www.peteducation.com/article.cfm?c=2+2084&aid=231>

"Cleaning Dogs Teeth." all about goldens. <http://www.all-about-goldens.com/dogs-teeth.html>

"Clipping Your Golden Retriever's Nails." zsoltm1778. <http://www.doggroomingtutorial.com/grooming-a-golden-retriever/clipping-your-golden-retrievers-nails/>

"Connective Tissue Tumors in Dogs." mypetMD.
<http://www.petmd.com/dog/conditions/cancer/c_dg_mast_cell_tumor#>

"Contrasting Grain-based and Meat-based Diets for Dogs." T.J. Dunn, Jr., DVM.
<http://www.petmd.com/dog/nutrition/evr_dg_contrasting_grain_based_and_meat_based_diets>

"Costs of Owning a Golden Retriever." Oxford Goldens.
<http://oxfordgoldens.blogspot.com/p/costs-of-owning-golden-retriever.html>

"Dog Breeding." Wikipedia.
<https://en.wikipedia.org/wiki/Dog_breeding>

"Dry, Semi-moist, or Canned Pet Food: What is Best?" Katharine Hillestand, DVM.
<http://www.peteducation.com/article.cfm?c=2+1659+1661&aid=3328>

"Elbow Dysplasia." Drs. Foster & Smith, Inc.
<http://www.peteducation.com/article.cfm?c=2+2084&aid=431>

"Games to Play With Your Golden Retriever Puppy." DogChannel.com.
<http://www.dogchannel.com/puppies/training/article_golden_retriever_2.aspx>

"Getting Serious about SAS." purinaproclub.com.
<https://www.purinaproclub.com/resource-library/todays-breeder/issue-76/getting-serious-about-sas>

"Golden Ears." Monique Lenczycki. <http://www.grr-tx.com/content/golden-ears>

"Golden Retriever." vetstreet.com. <http://www.dummies.com/how-to/content/is-a-golden-retriever-right-for-you.html>

"Golden Retriever." Wikipedia. <https://en.m.wikipedia.org/wiki/Golden_Retriever>

"Golden Retriever and Allergies." Carol Matthews. <http://www.streetdirectory.com/travel_guide/194049/pets/golden_retriever_and_allergies.html>

"Golden Retriever Dog Breed Profile." petplanet.co.uk. <pethttp://www.petplanet.co.uk/dog_breed_profile.asp?dbid=33>

"Golden Retriever FAQ: Frequently Asked Questions About Golden Retriever Dogs." Michele Welton. <http://www.yourpurebredpuppy.com/faq/goldenretrievers.html>

"Golden Retriever Grooming - What Tasks Need Doing?" Jet Parreault. <http://www.totallygoldens.com/golden-retriever-grooming/>

"Golden Retriever Showing." dogchannel.com. <http://www.dogchannel.com/dog-books/dog-breed-books/golden-retriever-showing.aspx>

"Golden Retriever study confronts heartbreak of cancer with unparalleled veterinary research effort." Jessica Vogelsang, DVM. <http://veterinarynews.dvm360.com/golden-

retriever-study-confronts-heartbreak-cancer-with-unparalleled-veterinary-research-effort>

"Golden Retriever Uveitis." Northwest Animal Eye Specialists. <http://www.northwestanimaleye.com/golden-retriever-uveitis.pml>

"Golden Retrievers." embracepetinsurance.com. <http://www.embracepetinsurance.com/dog-breeds/golden-retriever>

"Golden Retrievers and Obesity Issues." pets4homes.co.uk. <http://www.pets4homes.co.uk/pet-advice/golden-retrievers-and-obesity-issues.html>

"Golden Retrievers can have this one, heartbreaking flaw." D. Kim Smyth. <http://www.gopetplan.com/blogpost/golden-retriever-cancer>

"Grooming." GRCV. <http://www.grcv.org.au/Grooming.html>

"Grooming Your Golden." Golden Retriever Rescue of Mid--Florida. <http://www.grrmf.org/learn/grooming-your-golden/>

"Grooming Your Golden Retriever." absolutelygolden.com. <http://www.absolutelygolden.com/grooming-your-golden/>

"Hemangiosarcoma." Wikipedia. <https://en.wikipedia.org/wiki/Hemangiosarcoma>

"Hip Dysplasia in Dogs: Diagnosis, Treatment, and Prevention." Drs. Foster & Smith.

<http://www.peteducation.com/article.cfm?c=2+2084&aid=444>

"How Much Does a Golden Retriever Cost?" Golden Retriever Dog Club. <http://reliabletexaspower.com/how-much-does-a-golden-retriever-cost/>

"How Much Exercise Does a Golden Retriever Need." Wendy. <http://www.dummies.com/how-to/content/is-a-golden-retriever-right-for-you.html>

"How to Keep a Golden Retriever's Ears Healthy." zsoltm1778. <http://www.doggroomingtutorial.com/how-to-keep-a-golden-retrievers-ears-healthy/>

"How Much to Feed a Dog to Meet His Energy Needs." Drs. Foster & Smith. <http://www.peteducation.com/article.cfm?c=2+1659+1661&aid=2612>

"How to Feed a Golden Retriever." Kathy Partridge. <http://pets1st.com/articles/00021howtofeedagoldenretriever.asp>

"Identifying and Dealing with Allergies." Jim Wright. <http://www.totallygoldens.com/identifying-and-dealing-with-allergies/>

"Is a Golden Retriever Right For You?" Nona Kilgore Bauer. <http://www.dummies.com/how-to/content/is-a-golden-retriever-right-for-you.html>

"Large-Scale Cancer Study of Golden Retrievers Holds Hope for All Dogs." Jane Brackman, PhD. <

http://thebark.com/content/large-scale-cancer-study-golden-retrievers-holds-hope-all-dogs>

"Lymphosarcoma in Dogs." OncoLink.org. <http://www.oncolink.org/types/article.cfm?c=793&id=6020>

"Newborn Puppies." all about goldens. <http://www.all-about-goldens.com/newborn-puppies.html>

"Newborn Puppy Care." all about goldens. <http://www.all-about-goldens.com/puppy-care.html>

"Obesity in Golden Retrievers and How To Deal With It." Wendy. <http://www.totallygoldens.com/obesity-in-golden-retrievers/>

"Osteosarcoma." National Canine Cancer Foundation. <http://www.wearethecure.org/osteosarcoma>

"Owning a Dog Cost." costhelper pets & pet care. <http://pets.costhelper.com/owning-dog.html>

"Pigmentary Uveitis in Golden Retrievers." Eye Care for Animals. <http://www.eyecareforanimals.com/conditions/pigmentary-uveitis-in-golden-retrievers/>

"Preparing for Dog Birth." all about goldens. <http://www.all-about-goldens.com/dog-birth.html>

"Puppy Growth from Birth to 8 Weeks." all about goldens. <http://www.all-about-goldens.com/puppy-growth.html>

"Puppy Vaccination Schedule." Golden Retriever/Newfies. <https://sites.google.com/site/goldenretrievernewfies/puppy-vaccination-schedule-1>

"Puppy Vaccinations 101: What You Need To Know To Make Informed Choices." Andra Mircioiu. <http://www.totallygoldens.com/puppy-vaccinations-101/>

"Rescues listed by region." GRCA. <http://www.grca-nrc.org/localrescues.html>

"Responsible Breeding." AKC. <http://www.akc.org/dog-breeders/responsible-breeding/>

"Retriever (Golden)" CKC. <https://www.ckc.ca/en/Files/Breed-Standards/Breed-Standards/Group-1-Sporting/RTG-Retriever-Golden>

"The Five Most Important Items on a Dog Food Ingredients List." Dog Food Advisor. <http://www.dogfoodadvisor.com/choosing-dog-food/five-most-important/>

"Things to Know Before Owning a Golden Retriever." Samantha Sivils. <http://unsivilized.blogspot.com/2010/03/things-to-know-before-owning-golden.html>

"Thinking of Buying a Puppy? Find a Responsible Breeder." AKC. <http://www.akc.org/press-center/facts-stats/responsible-breeders/>

"What's in a Balanced Dog Food?" PetMD. <http://www.petmd.com/dog/nutrition/evr_dg_whats_in_a_balanced_dog_food>

"Whelping Puppies Problems to Watch Out For." all about goldens. <http://www.all-about-goldens.com/whelping-puppies-3.html>

"Whelping Puppies Stage Three Labor." all about goldens. <http://www.all-about-goldens.com/whelping-puppies-2.html>

"Whelping Puppies Stage Two Labor." all about goldens. <http://www.all-about-goldens.com/whelping-puppies.html>

Feeding Baby
Cynthia Cherry
978-1941070000

Axolotl
Lolly Brown
978-0989658430

Dysautonomia, POTS Syndrome
Frederick Earlstein
978-0989658485

Degenerative Disc Disease Explained
Frederick Earlstein
978-0989658485

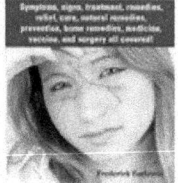

Sinusitis, Hay Fever,
Allergic Rhinitis Explained
Frederick Earlstein
978-1941070024

Wicca
Riley Star
978-1941070130

Zombie Apocalypse
Rex Cutty
978-1941070154

Capybara
Lolly Brown
978-1941070062

Eels As Pets
Lolly Brown
978-1941070167

Scabies and Lice Explained
Frederick Earlstein
978-1941070017

Saltwater Fish As Pets
Lolly Brown
978-0989658461

Torticollis Explained
Frederick Earlstein
978-1941070055

Kennel Cough
Lolly Brown
978-0989658409

Physiotherapist, Physical Therapist
Christopher Wright
978-0989658492

Rats, Mice, and Dormice As Pets
Lolly Brown
978-1941070079

Wallaby and Wallaroo Care
Lolly Brown
978-1941070031

Bodybuilding Supplements
Explained
Jon Shelton
978-1941070239

Demonology
Riley Star
978-19401070314

Pigeon Racing
Lolly Brown
978-1941070307

Dwarf Hamster
Lolly Brown
978-1941070390

Cryptozoology
Rex Cutty
978-1941070406

Eye Strain
Frederick Earlstein
978-1941070369

Inez The Miniature Elephant
Asher Ray
978-1941070353

Vampire Apocalypse
Rex Cutty
978-1941070321

www.ingramcontent.com/pod-product-compliance
Lightning Source LLC
Chambersburg PA
CBHW061949070426
42450CB00007BA/1099